P9-DEF-217

Christ and the Christian

CHRIST
and the
CHRISTIAN

by Robert W. Gleason, S.J.

SHEED & WARD — NEW YORK

Library of Congress Card Number 59–8237

Imprimi Potest:

Thomas E. Henneberry, S.J.
Praep. Prov. Neo Eboracensis

Nihil obstat:

John R. Ready
Censor Librorum
February 5, 1959

Imprimatur:

✠ Robert F. Joyce
Bishop of Burlington

Burlington, February 9, 1959

Manufactured in the United States of America

This book is dedicated to
Rev. Joseph O'Neill, S.J.,
for hope and encouragement.

Contents

Christ and the Christian

Introduction:

OLD AND NEW ORIENTATIONS

tieth-century man. Today the Christian finds in the inspired writings the authentic appeal of the word of God, truths naturally more vital than those of "devotional literature" as such. The spiritual life of our own period is thus developing through direct contact with the traditional sources of spirituality by employing means that were not accessible to other eras.[1]

St. Paul, for example, is being understood in a way quite different from that in which previous generations understood him. He has, indeed, become the "classical" spiritual author. Instead of a few isolated sentences or a few phrases reduced to scholastic terminology, it is his whole doctrine in all its force which now nourishes the spiritual life of the Christian.[2] The dogma of the Mystical Body of Christ has proved so rich a source of spiritual profit that perhaps no other doctrine has been so fully explored by contemporary asceticism.[3] Still another dogma brought into prominence by contemporary spirituality is that of the Resurrection. The dogmatic and spiritual significance of Christ's Resurrection as the climax of the redemption is now accented in a way that is even somewhat challenging. In the recent past one looked at the Resurrection from an almost exclusively apologetic point of view; today we see it as the final truth of salvation, vibrant with optimism and joy.

For centuries the Passion and Death of Christ had been favorite themes of Christian meditation, lending a certain tone to the whole of Christian devotion.[4] Today a new note of resurgent joy in redeemed humanity is clearly heard because we have a more complete grasp of the salvific importance of the Resurrection. Interest in the doctrines of the Resurrection and the Ascension of Christ has made us more fully aware of the importance, for the spiritual life, of Christian humanism, of the body and of marriage.

This century also is particularly appreciative of the deeper meaning of Pentecost in the Gospels and in the Epistles of St. Paul. The part played by the Third Person of the Blessed Trinity in the life of grace is increasingly the object of meditation and study. It is also noteworthy that the approach to the Last Things has undergone a certain shift in perspective. At one time the doctrines of Hell, Death and Purgatory were used mainly to quicken the salutary fear of the Christian and to rouse the sinner from his passivity. Today a new theme of hope has become integral to this part of theology, vitalizing the spirituality of the Christian with an entirely different atmosphere. Today, also, more attention is being devoted to the Parousia, the Return of the Lord, and to our hope for the promised new earth and new skies, the Jerusalem in which we will celebrate the marriage of the Lamb.[5] Although there is no opposition between the old and the new positions, the tone of each is different. The last century appreciated the clear, abstract note of speculative theology and emphasized the fact that we are unprofitable servants. Today we are returning increasingly to the concrete and encouraging words of our Lord to inspire us with hope for body and soul. This is a new Christian humanism.

It is also a fact that ascetical theology now accents the mystery of grace in quite a different fashion. A few decades ago it was customary to begin the theology of grace with a study of actual grace. As a result, actual grace became the dominant theme in devotional writing. The illuminations and other aids given the Christian to enable him to fight his battle courageously, to resist temptation, to quell concupiscence and to accomplish good works were prominently and fully discussed. Today, however, we are interested in the entire dogmatic synthesis of sanctifying grace, the foundation for the Christian life. As a result, habitual grace, the consequence of the presence of the Divine Trinity in our souls, is more widely commented on. The devotion of the faithful is moving in the same direction; it is habitual grace which the Christian seeks to understand, not that he wishes to ignore actual grace but because he realizes that it is ordained to habitual grace and is given for its preservation and growth.[6]

One cannot fail to notice also that an awareness of the reality of time, history, and the body has permeated Christian consciousness in a way that would have seemed strange to preceding generations. The entire liturgical revival, with its notion of gesture, of life, and of movement, makes clear how strongly a consciousness of the body has entered into our spiritual life. The missal now occupies its rightful place in Christian prayer, and the inspired psalms have replaced pious "prayer-books." The entire liturgical cycle has been renewed in beauty, intelligibility and profundity, and the Christian's sense of community is being rapidly developed. One can also remark a certain shift in the devotion of the faithful with regard to the Eucharist. The Mass is effectively understood for what it is in essence: the sacrifice of the community. Devotion to the Real Presence has been brought back to focus upon the Mass, the natural center of Eucharistic devotion. Rites which may have once seemed stylized and antiquarian have become powerful new influences in the lives of the faithful. Everywhere today the Christian is repeating the gestures of Christ in a renewed and revitalized liturgy.

We are also witnessing a renovation in the spiritual meaning of confession. There was a time when the role of the confessor seemed orientated rather more towards the role of questioner than toward that of listener. Today, however, the faithful look upon the sacrament of Penance less as a juridical exigency than as a humble approach to Christ, the judge and pardoner. Not only is it recognized as a reconciliation with God by means of the visible Church, but it is now more clearly understood as a source of vivifying contact with the person of Christ Himself, who renews within us the divine life of grace.[7]

Emphasis upon a theology of action has influenced all recent Christian spirituality. The great papal pronouncements dealing with Catholic Action in all its forms have served as an invitation to Christianize every aspect of existence. No longer is there question of the secularization of daily life with only Sunday devoted to the service of the Lord. Humanity today is more fully aware of its need for redemption through continual contact with God. A Christianity ever returning to the Scriptures is too serious, too profound and too demanding to remain on the margin of our daily life.

As a result the twentieth century is faced with a new problem, the meaning of Christian activity and work. On the one hand, Christian asceticism demands a retreat from what St. John called "the world," while on the other it urges us to represent Christ to the whole world. How are two such injunctions to be reconciled theologically? From the earliest days of Christianity there has been in the Church a stress upon withdrawal from the world in order to devote one's life to contemplation. Today, however, a deeper realization of the role of the laity in the Church and of the spirituality of marriage has clarified the need for the sanctification of every occupation and of every state of life. One either sanctifies them or one does not indulge in them. Thus the idea that marriage is something to be merely tolerated has now disappeared from Christian thought. Again, owing to the lack of a clearly formulated theological solution to the problem of action versus contemplation, Catholics have often withdrawn from political, economic and social life in order to cultivate their own souls. Today Catholics are aware that they must spiritualize their occupations and thus sanctify the institutions of the secular world. Whether it be educational, recreational, artistic, economic, political or international, the Christian has a role to play which may not be limited to a Sunday performance. This is the new accent of Christian devotion: the exploration of all values in the name of Christ and for the glory of God.[8]

With our new understanding of the redemptive activity of Christ spirituality has become more ecclesiological, rooted in the Church, and less individualistic. Not that present-day spirituality has dispensed with asceticism; this would be an impossibility in the Christian tradition. But asceticism is no longer devoted exclusively to the formation of a firm and solid will. Spiritual writers today have a deeper realization of the meaningfulness of simple prayer and of the primacy of grace in our relationships to God. Christianity is no longer in danger of being considered a kind of baptized stoicism instituted to correct our faults and to strengthen our wills. Instead it is thought of as an *agape*, a dynamism expanding the role of charity. Action today is seen as sanctifying because it is charity itself, within the bosom of Mother Church. The whole life of the Liturgy centers on the public and social adoration of God, fostering the community aspects of devotion.

Finally, another movement in contemporary spirituality has resulted in the death of Jansenism, or that form of moralism still popular in the nineteenth century which strongly accented the moral rather than the theological virtues. A stern sense of duty, a heavy emphasis on law, an overpowering fear, and an unbending rigorism had become prevalent in certain areas of nineteenth-century thought. Today, however, we stress the mystical elements of incorporation into Christ, divine indwelling, and divine friendship. The theological virtues are no longer considered inferior to pious acts, and charity rightfully occupies that supreme place in practice which it has always held in speculative theology. Intensive study of the dogmatic bases of the spiritual life has liberated souls from the stifling, cut-and-dried Cartesian atmosphere which at times lay heavy upon certain works of devotion in the past. As a result Christian souls today demand freedom of initiative and expect from their spiritual guides frankness, sincerity, and honesty. Technical and insipid routine no

Chapter 1

CHRIST THE CENTER

1

Christ the Center

It is important to observe that recent developments in spiritual theology represent not novelty and innovation but discovery and renovation. Fresh orientation has led us back to certain forgotten but rewarding springs. This return, however, has not involved forgetfulness of any of the central and perennial themes of Christian spirituality. Indeed, the distinctive characteristic of authentic Christian spirituality is precisely the way in which it keeps always in view the many facets of holiness, even as Christ our Lord perfectly harmonized in Himself the most disparate attitudes: meekness and strength, courage and tenderness, abnegation and accessibility. It is characteristic, too, of Christianity always to maintain a delicate balance between extremes and, without losing any part of a complex truth, to unite all elements in a synthesis which throws new light on the whole. The individual Christian is called upon to do something of the sort in his own spiritual life. His task is to tread a careful path between attitudes which, though apparently opposed, actually represent various aspects of truth. This necessity appears in perhaps its most basic form when the Christian finds himself confronted with the apparent conflict between the natural and the supernatural or between the accent of optimism and the accent of pessimism.[1]

OPTIMISM AND PESSIMISM

There is a sentence from the Gospel of St. John almost startling in its optimism. In the tenth chapter Christ the Lord, the Alpha and Omega of truth, gives us a summary of His mission. "I am come that they may have life and may have it more abundantly." In this direct utterance Christ explains the purpose of His existence as Incarnate Word, as God and Man, and He explains it in terms of an increase of life—surely an optimistic point of view. At times He phrased it somewhat differently, but the meaning was always the same: "It is not those who are in health that need the physician, it is those that are sick." And again: "The Son of Man is come to seek and to save that which was lost." But perhaps the clearest expression of His purpose in coming among us is this simple declaration: "I am come that they may have life and may have it more abundantly."

Into that one line Christ has compressed the whole spirit of Christian optimism. Yet it has taken philosophers and theologians many centuries to draw out the implications of these startling words. God has planned a new life for us; He has chosen to increase our capacity for living beyond anything we could imagine. In fact, He has planned for us an entirely new kind of life—the life of sanctifying grace.

The story of Christ's coming we call the Gospels; and the Gospels are the great and good news, the announcement of the definitive victory of this new life over death, over sin, and over Satan. For as the whole of human history centered in the momentous figure of Christ unfolds before us, we cannot but be aware of the happy position in which we Christians of these "last" days find ourselves. The victory belongs to the Christian. That is the meaning of Christ. The victory over death, sin and Satan is already ours, for Christ, our Victory, already exists and we have conquered in Him. The victory is ours, for we are not separated from the conquering hero but are closely united by mystical bonds to Him who has the victory, having gained it on Calvary. He is one of us, one of our race and family. His victory is ours, for He did not enter into it alone, but as the Head of the Body, His Church, of which we are members. The Head has already entered upon His triumph; and, if we but remain united to Him, our victory too is inevitable.

Nevertheless, life obviously has its dangers and difficulties, before which the Christian must take a realistic stand. Although traditional Christian asceticism will protect and preserve him, there still remain two fundamentally different attitudes towards life, the pessimistic and the optimistic.

The pessimistic attitude is negative, a dark and depressing view of things in which the victorious redemption of Christ appears to be kept in the shadows. It might seem as though such an attitude could never be part of lives that are authentically Christian; yet it is surprisingly easy to adopt such a viewpoint, particularly if one's theological perspectives are distorted.

Consider, for example, the way in which these two classes of souls approach the great mystery of God. The negative, pessimistic soul fastens at once upon certain isolated texts of Scripture which make God appear to be a hard taskmaster who reaps where He did not sow, and who lies in ambush among the shadows, ready to fall upon us in a moment of sin. To the negative soul God is an accountant, only too eager to show us our deficits in word and deed. A sorry picture, indeed, for if God were to play the auditor, very few of us would stand examination: "If Thou, O Lord, wilt mark iniquities; Lord, who shall stand it?"[2]

The attitude of the positive soul, the optimistic Christian, is quite different. He knows that God is the absolute Lord and Master, the unapproachably holy and just one, the transcendent, the totally Other. But he also remembers that God has recorded His own definition of Himself, "For God is love." It is a phrase from St. John, and St. John was neither pietistic nor particularly poetic. He was an incomparable theologian, the best of all the evangelists in this respect, and his definition is inspired. Although God is indeed a just God, He is also a *justifying* God through the free, undeserved gift of His grace. Although He is a demanding God, "a jealous God," He is never capricious or vindictive. His demands are ever-increasing, but they are all demands for more acceptance, for more readiness to receive the new gifts He has laid up for us. His demands are only the demands of one who loves.

Consider also the way in which these two classes of souls look upon man himself. To the pessimistic soul, man is essentially a spoiled creature, ruined, unbalanced, heavily laden with the effects of personal and original sin. Evil seems to triumph in him so often that hell appears to be inevitable, Satan the real victor, and man but a poor thing with a fallen nature.

"Fallen, to be sure, but redeemed," replies the optimistic Christian soul. It is folly to underrate the redemption of Christ. Satan is not triumphant. On the contrary, he went down to defeat on a certain hill outside Jerusalem and the victory of Christ is written large for all to see who have eyes to look upon a crucifix. Man is not a ruined creature, the helpless prey of Satan, but the spoils of Christ's victory. He is the prize of the redemption, won in the agony of Calvary, valued at a great price, bought not with the blood of oxen or of goats but with the blood of Him who is God.

In the center of all creation stands Jesus Christ, and with Him is the Christian. He and we are members of the same race, the same family, since Baptism has raised man to a quasi-equality with the God of the Old and of the New Testaments. Christianity is a family with a great tradition, and therefore the Christian has reason for optimism. For in his family are legions of martyrs, legions of virgins, legions of confessors, and all have placed their merits at his disposal in the unity of the communion of saints.

When we turn from the meaning of God and of man to the third great problem of the spiritual life, the meaning of creatures, we find the same contrasting attitudes. To the negative, pessimistic soul creatures are deformed and twisted beings, valueless in themselves, and merely tenuous instruments for our use. They are even to be feared lest they ensnare and destroy the unwary soul.

Genuine Christian insight, however, sees in creatures a meaning and dignity of their own. They are mirrors of God. The sacred humanity of our Lord is a creature; and, if it is a snare, it is a snare designed to catch and save us—that I may be caught by Christ, to echo St. Paul. We live in a sacramental universe in which all creatures tell of God. For they are the means God has chosen to form us as His children. It is true that they demand of us a wise and generous choice, but they are not evil. They have a role to play in our lives, and we have a role to play in theirs. Our task is to reconsecrate them to God and to rededicate them to Christ, the Center and Owner of all creaturedom. We are to bless them by our use and to stamp them with the image of the risen Lord. The Church, in furnishing special blessings even for such practical, mundane creatures as typewriters and fountain pens, is responding to the age-old appeal of creaturedom for its redemption. For the whole material world about us groans for the day of its liberation, and we are called upon to extend to it the effects of the redemption.

The two types of Christian we have been considering differ even in regard to the moral or spiritual life. For the negative soul the spiritual life is a long series of laws, an ever-expanding Decalogue. One must be wary of antagonizing a God who seems all too easily provoked to anger. Do nothing that can be punished, but there is almost nothing that is not tainted in some fashion, and therefore punishable.

Such a view is clearly imperfect. For the spiritual life consists above all in doing something and in being something. It consists in an expansion of our divinized life so that we may live for God, grow in His love, and make our talents fructify. Virtues are not negative dispositions. And prime in the Decalogue is the transcendent command "Thou shalt love the Lord, thy God."

The pessimist has an unrealistic view of God and the world, for he lives as though the redemption were incomplete. The optimist, on the contrary, is realistic because he takes into account both his own weakness and the power of God who has conquered the world. The pessimist's truth is only half a truth, and it needs to be completed with a real assent to the truth of the redemption, gloriously accomplished.

OUR LIFE IS CHRIST

Christian spirituality today is drawing from the rich deposit of faith certain virtualities which in recent ages were not so fully appreciated. But this is a process which must be carried on without detriment to that fine balance which is a hallmark of true Christianity. When we illustrated this point in the preceding pages by sketching the Catholic solution to the problem of the conflict between a spirit of optimism and a spirit of pessimism we indicated the pivotal truth which makes such a solution possible. This truth is not so much a doctrine as a person, for it is the reality of Christ our Lord which is the foundation stone of all our Christian optimism. Monsignor Romano Guardini has some burning phrases which illuminate movingly this fact of the centrality of Christ for Christian life, belief and behaviour. "If anyone should ask: What is certain in life and death—so certain that everything else may be anchored in it? The answer is: The love of Christ. . . . Only Christ's love is certain. We cannot even say God's love; for that God loves us we also know, ultimately, only through Christ. And even if we did know without Christ that God loved us—love can also be inexorable, and the more noble it is, the more demanding. Only through Christ do we know that God's love is forgiving. Certain is only that which manifested itself on the Cross. What has been said so often and so inadequately is true: The heart of Jesus Christ is the beginning and end of all things."*

It will be worthwhile, then, to dwell for a time on this theme of the centrality of Christ in all of life. It is, of course, a theme as old as Christianity itself, and the early Church felt it quite as poignantly as we do today. In the city of Ravenna stands the great Basilica of Santo Appolinare in Classe. In that sixth-century church there is a splendid mosaic of Christ the Redeemer dominating the center of the great arch—the Christ clad in gold and white, surrounded by the twelve apostles who draw near to him, emerging from the symbolic cities of Jerusalem and Bethlehem, the cities of the Old and of the New Testament—clear testimony that Christianity, from the earliest days, knew that the center of its faith was Christ Incarnate.

The centrality of the Incarnate Christ is the one fact which distinguishes Christians from all who are not Christians and which unites them among themselves.[3] The entrance of God into our temporal-spatial world is the heart of

***The Lord*, tr. Elinor C. Briefs, Chicago, Regnery, 1954; p. 400.

our faith. For in the Christian religion Christ is both founder and object. He is both initiator and content of the religion we profess. He is moreover the very element in which this religion is practiced, for Christ is the Church and the Church is Christ. Christ is the faith—the divine environment, the divine milieu in which our thought moves, our prayer ascends, our supernatural life unfolds. He is the content of our Christian religion, for every mystery of our faith unfolds fully only when it is related to this central mystery of the Incarnation of the Son of God. Christ is central to the Christian religion in a way that no other founder of a religion has ever dared to claim for himself.

Every religion has three elements, the intellectual element, the ritual or sacramental element, and the personal or mystical element. The intellectual element comprises what one believes in a religion, its dogmas or doctrines. The ritual element consists in those sacrifices and sacraments by which one comes closer to the divinity one worships, and the personal or mystical element is the individual life of the members of that religion in their relations to the God they adore. Now the Incarnate Christ stands at the center of each of these elements in the Christian religion. He is the intellectual element, for He is the dogmas that we believe. He *is* the Revelation Itself. He is the Word uttered by the Father that expresses all the reality of the God in whom we believe.

Moreover, Christ Incarnate, in His manhood and in His divinity, is the ritual or sacramental element in our religion, for the Sacrifice of the Mass is the real re-presentation of the Sacrifice He offered on a hill above Jerusalem.

The sacraments of our religion are the very gestures of Christ prolonged in time and space in His Mystical Body, the Church.

The historical Christ is also the center of our personal religious and mystical life. For He is the model, the perfect exemplar of all specifically Christian perfection. He is also the Interior Master who directs, suggests, restrains, molds, counsels and warns—in short, who forms our interior life. In an even more profound sense He is the center of our Christian life, for it is by His very life that we lead this spiritual and Christian life. In a real and supernatural sense He has inserted us into Himself, so that the very life that circulates in the Divine Trinity moves also in us. We live by His grace.

The theandric Christ, Christ God and man, is the center of our Christian religion not only because He is the center of its intellectual, ritual, and personal elements but also because He is the center of that original Revelation which the one true God made to man in the Old Testament. The Old Testament draws its meaning from Christ and reveals its fullness only in Him. Adam, the first man, prefigures the Christ, the First-born of many brothers who will be born anew to the life of grace. Moses, the great Lawgiver of the Old Testament, recalls to us the Christ who will free His people from the Law with its heavy and intolerable burdens and who gives us the new law of love and the liberty of the children of God. Joshua, the Liberator, points to Christ, who bought the Church in His blood, freeing us from the domination of sin. David, the great King, points to Christ, and Solomon, the Wise, points to Christ, and the entire Old Testament finds its fulfillment in the unique event that came to pass when God, remaining God, assumed also a true and perfect human nature.

In the New Testament the presence of Christ is all-pervasive. "What think you of Christ, whose Son is He?" This is the crucial question of the New Testament. It is the sum of the doctrine of the New Testament: "That you may know God and Him whom He has sent, Jesus Christ." It is the burden of the apostolic preaching. "I judged not myself to know anything among you, but Jesus Christ; and Him crucified." For Christ had made Himself the center of the lives of those who would follow Him. St. Paul expresses this truth in writing to his Ephesians: Once, he tells them, we were far off, we had no hope and were without God. "But now you are in Christ Jesus; now, through the blood of Christ, you have been brought close, you who were once so far away. He is our bond of peace. . . . You are no longer exiles, then, or aliens; the saints are your fellow-citizens, you belong to God's household." Christ Himself accepted from the people an adoration that placed Him at the center of their whole religious life, not once, but many times. Of Jairus, father of the dying child, of the Canaanite woman, of the mother of the sons of Zebedee, we read "and they worshipped Him."

Christ often demanded faith in Himself. We remember how He reproached His disciples in the storm-tossed boat: "O ye of little faith." And how He demanded hope in Himself: "Come to Me, all you that labor and are burdened, and I will refresh you." And finally, how in bold, uncompromising terms He demanded love of Himself: "He that loveth father or mother more than Me is not worthy of Me."

In a word, Christ made Himself the vital center of the Christian life. He has remained so in history, for the Lord Incarnate is the sign of the authentic Christian life. *Ubi Christus, ibi vita Christiana.* Even in the highest mystics the attachment to the Person of Christ in the flesh is central. St. Theresa of Avila reproaches Meister Eckhard, who would adore the Divine Trinity and by-pass the Sacred Humanity. It is the total Christ, Man and God, who is the beloved of the authentic mystic. Language itself expresses this centrality of Christ in our liturgical formula *per Christum Dominum:* one Mediator, Christ the Lord. In cult, life, and the entire Christian experience it is the Incarnate Son of the living God whom the Christian finds at the center of Christianity. The Latin races, without irreverence, have long named their children by His name to plant His memory within the very heart of the Christian personality. Christian art too, as we have seen, bears witness to this central role of Christ. Magnificent mosaics from the second and fourth centuries portray Jesus the Lord and Maker of all. Even earlier, the Roman Catacombs displayed their crude images of the Shepherd surrounded by His sheep.

The very earliest enemies of the Church perceived this unique quality and noted it in their descriptions of our faith. In the Acts of the Apostles, Festus, replacing Felix as Roman Magistrate about the year 60, warns Agrippa of the new religion and speaks of "a dead man called Jesus, whom Paul declared to be alive." That is the central fact of this new religion. Fifty years later Pliny the Younger describes Christianity as a cult addressed to Christ as to God. And this has been true of authentic Christianity through all the subsequent centuries. Where Christ is recognized as both God and Man we have the authentic Christian milieu.[4]

THE DREAD OF HEIGHT

Thus far we have dealt with certain broad lines of Christian spirituality and with certain great ideals which cannot but stir the most sluggish heart and nerve the most timid soul. The picture would not be complete, however, were we to omit certain more austere considerations which may diminish sentimental enthusiasm but can only strengthen genuine and solid spirituality. To begin with, there is the fact that sanctity has its own dialectic. It has its moments, its temporal invitations, its own rhythm of existence which cannot be ignored. We are not the lords of time, and we must accept the invitations of God in their own meaningful pattern.

Young souls, when first introduced to the spiritual life, are ordinarily eager for sanctity. Along with the native optimism of youth they generally have the good health, energy and drive to pursue sanctity almost as they would pursue any natural goal. More mature souls, however, are aware that acceptance of God's plan for sanctity involves dangerous and difficult demands. It is at this point that the soul experiences a feeling that could properly be called fear. It is normal for men to experience a sense of profound awe when the infinite approaches. Even our natural intelligence tells us that the demands of God may well be limitless. When the Christian realizes—as he ought to realize from the beginning of his Christian life—that genuine sanctity is the normal goal of his existence, he experiences a certain disquiet. At the encounter with One whose majesty is limitless, man begins to tremble as before an abyss. Who can measure the series of demands that God will make upon the soul destined to sanctity? Perfection is a terrifying word when spoken by God. The future, unrolling a panorama of splendid and terrible scenes, provokes anxiety. In addition, there lurks the ghost of uncertainty. Were God to reveal at once all the exigencies of His will, it is possible that man would dredge up the courage to obey even at the price of martyrdom. But the increasing pressure of God's insistent appeals to progress is a fearful thing to bear.

Many good men and women fear this pressing series of demands on the road to sanctity. They feel that their temperament fits them for a moderate life in which the extravagant, the ideal, the heroic have no place. It is normal for these less courageous souls to wish for a life full of moral virtues but to exclude the folly of the cross. Their fear, of course, is precisely that God's plan may not exclude this folly. But the moment they admit the possibility, *and* the desirability, of the cross, they alter their entire conception of life. Immediately, terrifying abysses open up before them, and the thought of a lifetime of trials and suffering almost paralyzes the mind.[5]

And yet, there is something in this invitation to be perfect which awakens a response within us. We know that the call of any great value demanding self-transcendence can energize us to our innermost being. We have all experienced such moments of response to an appeal issuing from a noble cause, and, submitting ourselves to its majesty, have felt ourselves more unified, more fully one with ourselves. On the other hand, we have also experienced the sadness of those whose world is well-regulated and secure but basically impoverished. For we do not easily accept a world whose dimensions are contracted. Even if the pattern of life is very clearly designed, we long occasionally for a generosity that would lift us above ourselves. Deep in our souls we know the truth of the words of Léon Bloy, "the only true sadness is not to be a saint."

Because our Lord has directed us to be perfect even as our heavenly Father is perfect, we can never halt upon the road, but must always continue to progress. At times we are led astray into meaningless detours through weakness of intellect and weakness of will. There are even moments when we defect ingloriously from the battle for God, and Satan celebrates a temporary victory. But at the same time we are drawn by the Spirit to our supernatural end, "holiness." The tragedy is that we resist the Spirit for so long. There are some who resist during an entire life, and perhaps only in the total option of death are really conformed to the crucified and risen Christ. Theirs is the "prudence of the flesh" which seeks to live in a sort of gilded mediocrity, carefully distributing themselves between spirit and flesh with a watchful eye on the future of both. A life of this sort can be pious and proper, "correct." But the Christian who remembers his origins knows that the fire and the spirit of the saints are conspicuously absent from so pallid an existence. The man in such a state still hears the ringing appeals of the Beatitudes, still realizes that God plans sanctity for him, still knows that the scope of God's command, "Be ye perfect," cannot be voided even by the most skillful casuistry. Eventually he becomes aware, even without formal instruction, that the deliberate resolve not to make progress in holiness is sinful and can even be gravely so.

Nor can one escape on the ground that he is not made for this type of heroism. Sanctity is precisely the reason for our existence. It is our destiny, and we cannot withdraw from it with impunity. We cannot substitute a plan for an adventure. What God calls us to is a risk, a commitment, a faithful giving over of self to His providence. What we often prefer is a series of well-defined and precise obligations whose observance will maintain us in His grace. The clearly established limits of law are obviously a bulwark to assure that inner security of which sanctity might deprive us. But it is just this climate of insecurity, this submission to an unforeseen and constantly changing set of circumstances, which shakes the soul. An inner malaise warns us that we are betraying our stronger desires. The call to a great vocation is not heard without troubling the deepest waters of our being. We may refuse to hear the call, but we do not thereby cease to be what we are by nature and grace, a spirit wholly polarized by the Infinite.

St. Augustine pointed out long ago that God has made us for Himself, and we shall not rest until we rest in Him. In denying His call to sanctity, we inevitably deny one of our fundamental longings as spirit.[6] For we are dynamized by the magnetism of His goodness. As long as we exist we will always be searching for that goodness. It is possible that we may be unaware of the authentic object of our search, but the search goes on. By nature this desire for the vision of God is conditioned, but through His grace we are made capable of possessing Him, and a new dynamism is at work within us. Our orientation towards Him is now the result of expanded capacities, and unless we fulfill these capacities, we are destined to confusion and unhappiness.

It could hardly be otherwise. We cannot check our movement towards God and remain in peace. We cannot diminish our appetite for the Infinite and succeed in satisfying our needs. We can pretend to be satisfied with less than the full and final good, but in the end, despite all attempts to diminish ourselves, we remain unsatisfied, lacking the total love that fills the aspirations of our hearts.

But love demands a Beloved, and so our thought returns once more to the Christian center, Christ our Lord. Christ is, indeed, not only the heart of our individual lives but the heart of all history, and He alone gives to history its meaning. The center of humanity, He reveals to humanity its destiny and ideal. It is He who unifies our understanding of the material universe, it is He who reveals to us the meaning and the value of the human person, and it is He who unfolds the relative significance of the temporal and the eternal, the human and divine.

The Christian must learn, then, to shift the focus of his preoccupations from himself to this unique model. He must learn to harmonize all things in Christ. Only then will Christ become the center of a personal relationship in which one member will be the human being and the other member will be the eternal God, and where the whole relationship will be one of love. *Unus est Magister noster, Christus.* We have but one teacher, Christ the Lord, the King and Center of all hearts.

Chapter 2

THE CHARITY OF CHRIST

2

The Charity of Christ

"God, who, at sundry times and in divers manners, spoke in times past to the fathers by the prophets, last of all, in these days, hath spoken to us by His Son . . . who being the brightness of His glory and the figure of His substance and upholding all things by the word of His power, making purgation of sins, sitteth on the right hand of the majesty on high." In these words of the first chapter of the Epistle to the Hebrews, St. Paul tells us that Christ our Lord is the Revelation of the Father. In Him we have not merely a new prophet, who will speak to us of God the Father, but we have God Himself revealing Himself to us, instructing us about Himself. We have God made visible and audible, God the Father revealed and made knowable in His Son, the perfect Image of the Father, the Brightness of the Father's glory and the Image of His substance. So much that we long to know about the great and hidden God who dwells in inaccessible light, we discover in gazing with the eyes of faith upon His visible manifestation, His incarnate revelation, His Son, our Lord and God.

GOD AND THE PHILOSOPHERS

Centuries before the advent of Christ men had pondered over the nature of God. Man's supreme desire has always been for union with God, and Christ the Lord is God's sublimest answer. For Christ reveals to us the very nature of God, so that we need no longer grope in darkness. In Him we behold the Father: "Philip, he that seeth me seeth the Father." "For the Father and I are one."

Prime among the truths that Christ has revealed about the nature of God and the essence of the Father is the truth that God is Love. The truth is not that God loves, but that God *is* Love, that Love expresses the very nature, the very essence of the Godhead. So accustomed have we become to this momentous fact that it has lost the power to open our hearts with wonderment, as it must have once opened the eyes of those to whom it was made visible in Christ our Lord. No mighty and piercing mind of the ancient world, however intuitive, had ever conceived the truth that the essence of God may be described by saying that God is Love. Aristotle, the greatest of the Grecian sages, had not dreamt it, for to him God is but an impersonal idea, the unmoved mover, the beloved of all, but Himself unable to love, for He is not a person. Nor had Plato, the most intuitive of all the ancient thinkers, ever conceived it, for Plato declares that the gods cannot love, since love reveals a need and the gods need nothing. Plotinus had not taught it, though Plotinus almost seems at one point to want to say as much.[1]

This truth, that God Himself is Love, dawned upon the

pagan world with shocking force at the advent of Christ. Always man had dreamed of ascending to God. Now, to the astonishment of the ages, God confirms man's most extravagant desires. God descends to man, revealing that He has love for man. St. Paul is so filled with this truth that it escapes from him in his letter to the Galatians like a cry of wonderment and exultation: "He loved me and delivered Himself up for me." And at the end of his life, writing to his beloved Ephesians, greeting them in what he thinks may be a last letter, he sends them what may well be his last blessing and expresses his dearest hope for them: "That, being rooted and founded in charity, you may be able to comprehend, with all the saints, what is the breadth and length and height and depth, to know also the charity of Christ." Then, as though astonished at the greatness of the thing he has just wished for his children, he adds the afterthought, "The charity of Christ, which surpasseth all knowledge." In the mind of St. Paul, who is here a first representative of Christian theology, the one essential doctrine of our faith in practice is the love of Christ for us, the love poured out upon man to manifest the nature of God, and the love by which He thus proved His own divinity.

THE GOD OF LOVE

God so loved the world as to give His only-begotten Son that the world might know this love and be made capable of responding to it. If we wish to grasp the secret of the mind and Heart of Jesus, we must look at Him in His function of revealer of the nature of the Godhead, the revealer of love. Once we have grasped this truth, we will see that every deed, thought and utterance of His Incarnate Majesty reveals it, dictated by that love for mankind which, St. John tells us, reflects the very essence of God. If we grasp this truth firmly, so that all other truths as well as all the circumstances of our lives are interpreted in its light, we are approaching an understanding of our Lord, the Revelation of God. This truth, that the very nature of God is love, should be the ultimate motive force for our patience, for our kindliness, for all our energy in doing the daily and often unrewarding tasks that fall to us. And once we have made it the motivating force of all our actions, we will know liberation from the dragging weight of discouragement, timidity and passivity.

From the first moment of our Lord's career the warmth and lovability of His nature was revealed. On the banks of the Jordan He drew His first disciples with the simple words, "Come and see." No argument, no dialectic: the revelation of who and what He is draws them, the incomparable charm of His Person, of a heart that knew no motive save love. With the apostles, with Nicodemus, with the Samaritan woman at the well, this amazing power to draw all men to Himself is brilliantly manifest. Did not the crowds follow Him, pursuing Him to the very water's edge, following Him even to the desert, even to the point of hunger and thirst? Moved by a consciousness of His personal interest in them, they wondered at the inexhaustible stream of love that radiated from Him. He heals the sick, restores sight to the blind, cures the sinful of their sins, and always the same attentive gaze is directed upon the individual.

A person-to-person love is established between Him and each of the many who come to Him. When at the house of Peter's mother-in-law, although weary from the events of the day Jesus is called upon to cure the whole village of its sick, the Evangelist specifically notes for us how He did it: "On each he puts his hands." This is no detached social reformer, no cool, impersonal physician: this is one who knows how to love, whose love is inexhaustible, identified with His very Person, for He is God, and God, as St. John tells us, is Love.

He spends His life in doing good, moving with majestic choice towards the great proof of love, His passion, consummating His work and manifesting the eternal love of God with the simple words: "It is finished." No man has ever loved or will ever love as Christ did. That is why, when the Corinthians are quarreling over their favorite leaders, some saying that they belong to Apollo, who has worked with them, some that they belong to Cephas, some to Paul, Paul silences them with a brutally revealing question: "Was Paul, then, crucified for you?" Greater love than this no man has than to lay down his life for his friends. And Christ laid down that life, not for humanity in the abstract, but for each person, individually known and loved. Even with His human mind Christ knew from the first moment of His earthly career each soul in the course of history who would share in the benefits of His redemption.

The love that He revealed for our imitation is remarkable for two qualities, strength and tenderness, the deepest tenderness and the most heroic strength. It is a love that never fears to rebuke—that never shrinks before obstacles, that bears with constancy betrayal and contempt, that is not weakened even by the certitude of failure. And it is a love that is genuinely tender and human. Each soul that meets the Lord is treated as unique. The Lord is the perfect humanist, knowing how to measure His treatment according to the personal characteristics of each. John is not treated as Peter, Peter as Andrew, Andrew as Philip. The particular love that Christ bore them is made concrete in His kind and affectionate way of dealing with each. Even more striking is the identification of Himself with all men, even His "least brethren."

CHARITY IN THE OLD TESTAMENT

It is because of this new union which Christ has established between Himself and the Christian that His command of charity is new. The Old Testament had insisted upon charity towards one's neighbor, but in a very restricted sense. In obedience to the attitude of God Himself, who was concerned with the poor, the devout Israelite showed charity to the members of the kingdom of the elect. But those outside the kingdom of Israel were considered impious and destined for destruction. Israel constantly displayed its vehement concern for the dispossessed of this world, the poor, the foreigner adopted by Israel, the widow and the orphan. But a very sharp religious nationalism shut Israel off from charity towards all others. Israel had heard the command of God: "When thou reapest the crops on thy land, do not rase all to the level of the ground, or pick up the scattered ears; do not hoard up the clusters or the grapes that have fallen. Leave something for poor men and wanderers to glean; *remember what God you worship.*" Israel was to imitate the divine mercy toward the poor and the oppressed. Yahweh is pleased with a heart of flesh, Isaias tells us: "Share thy bread with the hungry, give the poor and the vagrant a welcome to thy house; meet thou the naked, clothe him; from thy own flesh and blood turn not away. Then, suddenly as the dawn, the welcome light shall break on thee, in a moment thy health shall find a new spring; divine favour shall lead thee on thy journey, brightness of the Lord's presence close thy ranks behind. Then the Lord will listen to thee when thou callest on Him; cry out, and He will answer, I am here at thy side. Banish from thy midst oppression, and the finger pointed scornfully, and the plotting of harm, spend thyself in giving food to the hungry, relieving the afflicted; then shall light spring up for thee in the darkness, and thy dusk shall be noonday; the Lord will give thee rest continually, fill thy soul with comfort, thy body with ease. Not more secure the well-watered garden, the spring whose waters never fail." Israel understood that if she was to imitate her God, the supreme manifestation of morality, she must imitate Him in mercy and charity towards all of Israel.

CHARITY IN THE NEW TESTAMENT

Only much later did Christ expand the Israelite idea of charity to a universal charity; only much later did Israel understand that God was the Lord of all creation, that He summoned all people to adore Him and exercised His providence and charity over all. The love Christ calls us to have for all men is a distant imitation of the universal love of God revealed in the universal redemption in Christ. "Beloved, if God has shown such love to us, we too must love one another. No man has ever seen God; but if we love one another, then we have God dwelling in us, and the love of God has reached its full growth in our lives."

The New Testament reveals the love of God for mankind in a completely transcendent fashion. When Christ spoke of the Fatherhood of God, He uttered a basic new word concerning God, for although God was at times called Father in pre-Christian religions, His paternity was usually conceived as material. Generally speaking, the Fatherhood of God was a pure metaphor applied to God because He was the creator. God was Father to objects as well as to persons—a concept completely foreign to the New Testament. In the Old Testament God revealed Himself as Father to the whole people, but His fatherhood of the individual was not stressed.[2]

It was only with the New Testament and Christ's revelation of the Trinity that man fully grasped the notion of God's love and of His Fatherhood to each man. For the Trinity is a mystery of the highest union and at the same time of distinction of persons. The very life of the Godhead consists in the divine processions by which a divine person communicates to another the divine nature with which both persons are identified. Thus there is, at the very origin of being, a total donation of self, love. The relationship between the persons of the Trinity is of ineffable intimacy, since the only distinction among them is the relative distinction founded upon origin. Thus it is that the Father gives all that He possesses, save the relationship of paternity itself, to the Son, and from the Father and Son proceeds the Holy Spirit, identical in nature and absolute attributes with themselves. The Holy Spirit is subsistent love. It is out of love that the Father has given Christ the glory of the Father and given it to Him from eternity. (John 17:24.) The relationship which exists between Father and Son is not merely based upon love; it is love itself. Thus, when St. John defines God as love, he is speaking of the inner life of the Trinity and openly states that trinitarian life consists in love. It is because God is love in Himself that St. John introduces this idea of the manifestation of the divine love toward us; the relation of the Trinity to mankind is a relationship of love which seeks to introduce men into union with the Trinity, and to give them a share in Its life.

LOVE OF NEIGHBOR

There are some Christians who seem to believe that the affection they should have for their fellow Christians or for their family is a sort of detached neutrality. The early Christians, who lived by the tradition handed down from the apostles, did not so interpret Christian love. They knew it as a source and creator of unity—experienced unity. "See how they love one another," the pagans wondered. Reading the history of the primitive Church, we observe how a Christian was beloved by other Christians because he was a Christian. This new gospel dissolved all barriers of class, education, taste and race. One cannot but wonder how fully we understand the Christian gospel today. This was the gospel that astounded the pagan world by proclaiming a God who was love and then went on to further astound the world by proclaiming a mystical, supernatural but real identity of the Christian with God Himself, so that the logical consequence was, "Whatever you do to the least of these you do to me." The early Christian took this quite seriously, as a good theologian must, and it brought to his life incomparable richness and joy, a wealth of universal, supernatural love in the fullest sense of the word. But such a sense is utterly foreign to our modern pale and washed-out concept of love.

The reader has no right to change the clear and open meaning of Sacred Scripture. Christ revealed to us that He is Love, that the Father is Love, that the Holy Spirit is subsistent Love, and that this love is operative with regard to us personally. We may not then interpret love as "like," but must so penetrate this truth and absorb its meaning that it energizes our personal life, banishing discouragement, timidity, coldness and indifference. The Christian's work is successful precisely in the proportion that he brings to it a reflection of this honest human love of Christ for each soul that He touches. If we have so depersonalized our relation with God that the Christian life has become for us primarily a set of impersonal rules and obligations, then we must re-personalize our lives with God, deepening our realization of the truth that God is Love, that this love is directed to us, and that it calls to us for a response of love. One of the great signs of the coming of Christ was that the poor had the gospel preached to them. One of the most triumphant signs of the continuation of

Christ's love on earth is the fact that the little ones of this world, the children, the poor, the neglected, still have the gospel preached to them by other Christians. To penetrate this apostolic work with love, to realize that this work is an extension of the redemptive love of Christ working through us, is part of our task.

This can be done only to the extent that we grasp what Christ has revealed: the essence of God is love, and that as it was His task to reveal to the world the nature of God by His sacrificial activity, so it is the Christian's task to continue that revelation to a world grown disbelieving in the very possibility of sacrificial love. It was His function to bear witness to the nature of the Father. It is the Christian's committed task to witness to the Son, love made manifest, by a life of sacrificial love—not merely by service, but by love for the Church and its members, mystically, really identified with Christ—"For whatever you do to the least of these" you do to Christ.

GROWING TO THE STATURE OF CHRIST

The Christian must realize too that Christ's command to love is in accord with man's essential nature as a limited creature. Like all the demands of God it tends to expand our own potentialities, and is no external curb capriciously placed upon liberty. Love aims at our self-development. For man is most himself when, transcending egoism, he gathers up all his energies in that full self-possession which results only from long effort and makes the gift of himself to another. For each man is naturally and closely related to all others, and he must reach out in love towards them to fulfill his own nature. The human person, like all created existence, is a faint and distant echo of the relational character of the Blessed Trinity. Man must, if he is to be true to himself, live out this relational character in all human contacts.[3]

My love for others, then, is a necessity for personal development. For me to grow to the adult stature of Christ I must fully possess my own being that I may then give it away. Insofar as I am closed and incommunicable to others, unable to set up human relationships of love with them, my own existence is diminished in quality. I live then in a depersonalized world of objects, and the temptation comes to treat others as external obstacles to my progress. But spiritual beings are not susceptible of treatment at the level of matter. They do not respond to the same laws as do material objects; brutal thrusts and pulls can never establish that human character in man's relationships which enables him to live in peace with himself. Men have their own proper being and their own proper subjectivity which Christian humanism demands that we find and appreciate as an original source of liberty. Only then can I give up the manipulation of other individuals as objects to be acquired or crushed, and instead find in them the same openness to communion that I seek for myself.

The Church herself is objectively the supreme communion of all men, and it is she who holds out to us the final possibility of development for our human personalities in the communion of saints. This communion of saints is itself closely allied to the beatific vision, where we shall share the joy of all humanity come to its consummation through contact with the Trinity. My own humanity is impoverished when I am unable to reach others with a gesture of love. The greatness of the moral personality of Christ is summed up in the phrase of St. Paul, "the goodness and the *humanity* of God, Our Savior, have appeared." I frustrate my deepest tendencies when I live in an isolated individualism surrounded by a world of objects without depth or subjectivity.

The breath of divine charity should, then, inform all our human love, for Christ, the perfect humanist, suppresses nothing of value in human life. Instead He elevates and enriches all that is good in human affection. Consequently, all our loves should be an expression of divine charity. Love of friendship, of art, of nature, of our family, whatever the type, it should exist in Christ and with Christ, as an expression of our dedication to God. To say that charity is a divine virtue is not to say that it is an inhuman one. There is nothing authentic in human love which suffers at the hands of this divine virtue. On the contrary, charity is as a form infusing and vitalizing the matter of every genuine human love.

Divine charity seizes upon our human affections as they exist in the concrete, historical order and unites them in the unity of Christ. Human love is thus transfigured and unified by the virtue of charity, but never distorted nor stifled by it. Failure to understand this has often caused difficulties and misunderstandings in the matter of our love for one another. Charity itself should intensify all that is legitimate, transposing it to a divine level, but it should in no sense chill, desubstantialize or truncate human affectivity.[4]

LOVE, FALSE AND TRUE

While it is true that Christ demands that we love men as a pledge of our love for Him, we have seen that He does not mean that we are to treat men with an impersonal kindness which disregards their intrinsic and individual lovability. Nor does he mean that we are to love men purely for a quality extrinsic to them. One sometimes hears fraternal charity explained thus: Since God has adopted mankind, we are to treat His adopted children as though they were His real children, a prolongation of the divine personality. But this sort of reasoning resembles too closely an artificial juridical fiction, and divine adoption is far more than a juridical fiction. Divine adoption actually alters the interior of man, establishing within him, in the objective order, a family resemblance to the divine Trinity. Men are thus truly sons of God. This false concept of fraternal charity is also dangerous in that it tends to by-pass the intrinsic good of the one loved and to direct one's attention solely upon God. This would not be authentic charity because man is, through God's goodness, a genuine value in himself. All creatures have their own worth and demand from us a respect and a love fitted to their dignity. The intrinsic greatness of man can be known by natural reason, which demands that we love him for what is actually in him through the creative action of God. Surely the charity of Christ is not less human than natural charity.

We love our neighbor because he has within himself the

Holy Spirit and the divine gifts of grace. Yet it is not only grace that we love in him, for grace is essentially reflective of God and oriented towards a Divine Person. Grace is the effect of the communication of the very substance of God, the effect of the donation of God's very being to the substance of the human soul. One who loves another because of the supernatural gifts with which God has endowed him actually loves God within him, for the whole of grace is directed towards the transcendent Giver. It is thus that in loving man one loves God, who communicates His grace to man. In loving man because of his supernatural gifts we cannot abstract from the Source of them all. Were we to do so, it would not be theological charity at all. Theological charity demands that we love *God in the neighbor*.

Nevertheless, one must beware of interpreting this as though we should use others as a means to love God, as though mankind were a functional channel through which we arrive at God. The human person has a dignity in himself and must not be used as a simple means. Human beings justly resent this form of so-called charity in which they are merely instruments in the unhappy efforts of the lover to improve his moral status. We respect men and we find God Himself in them. Our charity is genuinely addressed to the man who confronts us and to his intrinsic worth. Since God has made Himself one flesh with humanity, humanity is exalted. We can seek God within its bosom and need not pass through humanity to seek the Source of man's divinization. Fraternal charity directs itself at what is most personal, individual and profound in the human person.

But precisely what *is* most personal and profound in human nature is Christ Himself, who possesses the ultimate secrets of every human personality and sustains in existence that created act of personality which renders each of us singular, individual, incommunicable—ourselves. So it is that this virtue is at once completely human and at the same time divine. In loving the neighbor, charity seeks God, and has God as the formal object of its action. We love God realistically within the neighbor because God is actually found there. Moreover, God dwells within the neighbor not inertly as in a temple, but actively, forming the conscience of the neighbor, elevating him to the divine order, and rendering him lovable by divine charity. It is a highly extrinsic fashion of viewing things to think that we make God the formal object of our charity towards the neighbor simply because God has commanded that it should be done. For us to fail in love of the neighbor after God has commanded us to love him would be a failure to love God Himself. Doubtless a soul which understands the identification of Christ with humanity will seek to fulfill in every detail the invitation of Christ to treat all men as Himself. But on the other hand, we must not empty this divine message of all realism and ontological meaning and consider it as a merely legal procedure ordered by God. God's orders are always an affirmation of reality.[5]

Charity is not an easy virtue; it demands mortification and renouncement. Were this not so it would not be a divine virtue, but only another miserable caricature of Christian virtue. When charity fulfills its own inner demands for heroism through obedience, poverty, chastity or renouncement, we see clearly that this virtue is no mere intensification of human loves, but is at once divine and human, theandric and incarnational. For while it is fully human, responsive to the secret exigencies of the soul, and humanizing the man who practices it, at the same time its unique formal object is divine. It is divine in excellence and perfection. It is just as essential as love directly borne towards God, for the Christian life is itself theandric and incarnational. Since the day when God united Himself to man, fraternal charity has become an intrinsic necessity. Christ revealed this necessity by coming to earth, but it is a necessity which responds to an implicitly natural vocation within the soul itself. By becoming hypostatically united to human nature, Christ divinized humanity and lent it a reflection of His own lovability. Charity now explores the depth of humanity until it comes into contact with the living God, whose lovability makes humanity lovable in itself.

The love of our fellow men is, as we have seen, in some sense a reflection of the reciprocal relations which eternally exist within the Trinity. Because the Eternal Spirit is the love between Father and Son, fraternal charity is constantly associated with Christ in Sacred Scripture. As the Eternal Father shows forth His love for mankind in Christ, who is the witness and the sacrament of the Father's love for mankind, so the Christian with his new heart of charity has the capacity to love all men in imitation of the unlimited goodness of God. The Christian is thus another Christ witnessing to love of the Father for mankind. He seeks out in the person of each of his brethren the mysterious presence of the Eternal Son, and the fullness of the Godhead which dwells corporally within Him. It is no human power which enables us to love our brethren, but a share in the inner life of God Himself. We share in the trinitarian exchanges through grace, and it is thus that we are able to have a heart of flesh and give testimony to love of mankind for Christ, and in Christ for God.

A triumphant hymn of love rises to God from within the heart of needy humanity which has been empowered to love by His Spirit diffusing His charity in our hearts. The Father, glorified in Christ, who progressively unites to Himself the whole of humanity, is loved in all Christians, who progressively invade the whole of humanity with fraternal charity. Christ in humanity offers to God a distant reflection of the eternal love which binds Father and Son in heaven. Our love for our brethren is the sign, during the last times, the days of the Church, of the love that unites Son to Father. As Christ is the last sign given by God, the full revelation of His Mystery, the perfect and infinite Word to which no word can be added, the human revelation of the divine, so the Christian is the presence of Christ to fallen humanity. God manifested His love for us by sending His only-begotten Son into the world. The love, in turn, of Christ for His Father is manifested in the Christians' love for the Father and for each other. It is our task as Christians to imitate that supernatural generation by which we are made sons of God. As the Father from all eternity utters one Word, generates one perfect Son and Image, so too the Christian by his charity and delicacy towards the neighbor brings to birth in the neighbor the image of God. It is only by such activity that the Christian manifests that full *humanitas* of which St. Paul speaks: "*humanitas Dei apparuit.*"[6]

The high dignity of this charity is clear when we recall that it has ordered to it even the supernatural moral virtues. For these become incarnational and Christian insofar as they are an expression of divine charity. From this we can deduce what a central role fraternal charity occupies in human life. It is this virtue which enables us to open the deepest strata of our souls and meet in communion with others on that level where our decisive options are made. Since it is only Christ who grasps the ultimate themes of every soul, our deepest human contact with others, destined to mature us personally, can be made only in Christ. Unless we fully enter into Christ and into the great stream of love that bears Him and redeemed humanity towards God, we are cut off from the fullest measure of understanding, sympathy and unity in our human contacts. It is impossible to love God without at the same time loving man, and it is impossible to love man properly without at the same time loving God, for what we seek for man is his blessedness, the same beatific vision we desire for ourselves and God wills for us. This is the open communion which the Church, the sacrament of Christ, establishes among all men.[7]

CHRIST IN HIS BROTHERS

Theologians have long reflected upon the particular manner in which Christ may be said to be "identified with the Christian." Our Lord Himself has stated it very realistically in His description of the decisions handed down at the Last Judgment and in such statements as these: "Whatever you do to the least of these, you do to me," "He that receiveth you, receiveth me." Neverthless this union between Christ and the Christian is not easy to clarify. Certainly it is much more than a merely moral union such as binds two human friends who share thoughts, aspirations and affections. It is not merely a union in the order of intention, idea or affection. Yet neither is it a hypostatic union in the sense that the Christian surrenders his personal identity to be somehow blended into a pantheistic synthesis with Christ. Sanctifying grace, the bond that unites us to Christ, is itself not in the moral order but in the quasi-physical order, since it exists independently of the operation of the mind. Yet it is difficult accurately to explain in philosophical terminology those vigorous Pauline affirmations of Christ existing in the Christian and the Christian existing in Christ. For our purpose it is sufficient to realize that each one of my fellow men mysteriously represents Christ and is a sign of His presence. Since he is in some fashion identified with Christ, my neighbor's deepest strata are accessible only in Christ. In the present order I find Christ in the Church, the sign and the mystery of Christ and of God, and in fraternal charity.

Charity is essentially a realistic virtue since it accepts man's fundamental situation concerning God and the entire universe. Man is not an isolated being cast into existence to work out his destiny alone. He is from the beginning a member of the human society, and by vocation, at least, a member of the Mystical Body of Christ, the supernatural community related to this entire universe. To be fully himself, man must live out this dependent and relational character of his being not only with regard to all mankind but indeed, in a certain sense, to the material universe itself. The more united to God is man, the more he is united to humanity and to this world which is humanity's destined framework. The more united he is to others, the more fully he gives himself in all his autonomy and originality, the more completely human does he become.

SUMMARY

The initiative of God is brought home to us most closely in the primal grace of gift, Christ Himself. He is the offering of love sent by God to mankind. When man by faith and grace accepts this divine offer, then his life becomes wholly one of love. Fraternal charity is then an expression of faith itself, for as St. Paul points out, the thing that matters for the Christian is the faith that expresses itself in charity, a submission to God and a union with Him in the brethren. When Jesus spoke of the Golden Rule and of the need for fraternal charity He linked it very closely to participation in the life of the Trinity. Man, if he is to be a son of God, must imitate God's love for humanity and share in the designs of God for humanity. For St. Paul, as for the writers of the synoptic Gospels, Christians are called upon to imitate Him whom they call Father, by imitating His love for mankind. St. Paul says quite clearly that we imitate God by imitating Christ. We fulfill the old and the new law through fraternal charity because this precept of charity replaces all the rubrics of the old law and induces a new imitation of the deity who calls us sons.[8]

The incessant appeals of St. John for charity are based upon this same theology of sonship. Whoever loves his brother has done all that God asks of him, for he has imitated God in Christ and fulfilled his vocation to sonship. The whole vocation of the Christian is involved in this notion of sonship and is fulfilled when man lives as son. It is for this reason that St. John can appeal to man's love for mankind to prove man's union with God. Since God is love, if we bear this love to one another, then the proof is clear; we have received it, as a free gift from Him who owns it naturally. We are living the life of God, imitating the God who loves us as a Father. We abide in God and God in us, as God abides in the Son and the Son in Him, if we live by this charity—benevolent, disinterested, universal.

Put in this setting, the highpriestly prayer of Christ for union at the Last Supper takes on new meaning. It becomes clear in this setting of fraternal charity that the union between Christians demonstrates the divinity of Christ and His Church, for they make it evident to the world that they are living the life of God and are therefore from God. Christ must have come from God, and the Church must be of God, if within it one finds the life of God: charity.

Christians are called to imitate the trinitarian exchanges, for they too are supposed to give, not merely of their possessions but of their own hearts to "the brethren." Within the Trinity the three persons communicate in the one numerically identical nature. They eternally give themselves to each other and thus constitute a most total union within a distinction of persons. Our fraternal charity is a reflection of this life. God within us gives Himself to the neighbor, and we, in Him, are empowered to give ourselves. We, therefore, do not merely *serve* the neighbor; we give of ourselves. So true is it that we actually touch God in the neighbor, that the New Testament from time to time even uses the word *agape* to designate fraternal charity. Since *agape* refers to a love which is active and efficacious in giving, it might seem impossible that we could love God with *agape,* do Him good, give gifts to Him. Yet, the one who loves his neighbor fulfills the duty which he has as a son. Living the life of the Father, loving as a son, he can show to God a genuinely disinterested and an efficacious love in loving the neighbor. Love of the neighbor is thus a certain sign, perhaps the only certain sign, of our love for God, the proof that we have passed from death to life and been established in the kingdom of His Son, for it is only by this love that we efficaciously love God, with *agape.*[9]

The communal life of the early Church reflected this doctrine of the mystical identity of Christ and Christian. But charity becomes more universal as mankind understands better the nature of God Himself. Although its ultimate source is always the trinitarian relations, its most complete manifestation is the baptism of the cross. After such a revelation the Christian understands that he must accept on faith the identity of Christian and Christ. Again, charity makes us servants of one another (Gal. 5:13), because our ultimate longing is to be the servant of God Himself. When men behold this unity of Christians they learn something of the Father's love for humanity and the love of the Son

Chapter 3

THE SUFFERING OF CHRIST

3

The Suffering of Christ

All the lines of our spiritual life converge upon Christ, the central fact of Christianity. We must never cease our effort to know Him more fully, for Christ is the very Revelation of God. When we observe His acts we are observing the acts of God. When we observe His attitudes we are observing the attitudes of God. In Him the invisible God has come within the reach of creatures, so dependent upon the visible and the tangible. It follows, then, that we must go humbly and reverently to Christ, our suffering Redeemer, to learn the meaning of suffering. If we try to study suffering apart from the figure of the great suffering Redeemer, it will be unintelligible.

Moreover, the cross of Jesus is not only the deepest answer to the question posed by human suffering, but it is also a mighty source of light on the meaning of man. For the Greek, the man without faith, suffering is indeed a scandal, an evil to be avoided at all costs, the one thing in the universe that seems completely meaningless. For the Jew, the cross is a stumbling block. That is to say, the man who has a preconceived idea that human greatness consists in honor, glory, power, riches, will never be able to accept the fact that the author and finisher of our faith, Jesus Christ, divine and total Wisdom, chose the cross. But Paul goes on to tell us that for the Christian the cross is the power and the wisdom of God Himself. We must, therefore, try to achieve the perspective of the Christian in the matter of suffering.

What is conspicuous in both Scripture and Tradition is the fact that Christ did not seek suffering for suffering's sake. All the classical doctors of theology are unanimous upon this point. St. Thomas has expressed it beautifully: God the Father permitted the Passion, God the Son accepted the Passion, and the Holy Spirit infused in the holy soul of Jesus that charity which inspired Him to His Passion.

The will of the Holy Trinity was directed towards those interior acts of self-donative love by which Christ the Man honored the entire Trinity and opposed Himself to the loveless rebellion of sinful humanity. It was love which achieved our redemption, love which expressed itself in this particular form of suffering because of the conditions of humanity. Because matter is inert and because human nature and the external world offer opposition to our objectives we must frequently obtain them in suffering. So it was with Christ. He did not find within Himself those resistances to love which we find, but outside Himself He met with great resistance: inertia, apathy, lack of comprehension, indifference, hatred, and tepidity. All these attitudes Christ experienced, and in translating His plan of love into action He needed to encounter suffering. Jesus sought this suffering, not because it had a value in itself, but because it was a way to translate His charity into act. In resisting those who would prevent the translation of His love into the external world Jesus suffered, and accepted suffering willingly. And always before His mind was the objective He pursued: to break the power of sin, to bring about the reign of redemptive love through the entire world.[1]

THE CROSS AND THE CHRISTIAN

God has need of men to continue His redemptive work. Because Christ redeemed the universe but did not impregnate it with His redemptive love, we must accept the task of extending the reign of His charity. In doing so we take up the battle, with the assistance of His grace, to redeem the universe. The cross and suffering are signs of love in a double sense: they prove the existence of love and they themselves, like many signs, have no meaning apart from the thing they signify—charity. In our suffering we do not merely copy externally the attitudes of Christ. Rather we remold ourselves according to His design of extending the realm of redemptive charity throughout the world. In doing so we encounter suffering, but suffering is always at the service of our objective—charity. At times we must seek suffering actively, because without it we cannot cause Christian love to penetrate external reality; without suffering we cannot extend the kingdom of God. Ultimately the important thing always is that charity which should form all our virtues. Because of this charity, suffering has advantages both for ourselves and for others. In us it extends the domain of Christ, teaching us patience and humility, and it is a source of encouragement for those who witness our sufferings, if we suffer in the spirit of Christ.

It is useless even to attempt to comprehend the Christian attitude to suffering unless we hold firmly to this truth: the cross was not forced on Christ by certain Jews or Romans. It was chosen by Christ as the preferable way over several other means of redemption. He chose the cross with measureless, limitless, unimaginably total freedom, with the freedom of God Himself.

Faith in the figure of Christ on the cross teaches us several consoling truths. The first truth is that suffering is by no means a sign of abandonment by God. The Old Testament Jews thought that it was, but they had not beheld the Crucified who is the sum of Christian wisdom. Christ transformed suffering, not by a declaration, but by a deed, by his situation on the cross. It is the *beloved* Son who is crucified, and this will always be true of us, His continuation, His prolongation, His mystical body.[2]

The sight of Christ suffering teaches us to ignore the human circumstances that seem to cause the suffering in our lives. Actually, the cause of my suffering is not this person, this event, this deficiency in myself; rather is it the Lord God who permits my suffering. It is foolish and demoralizing to focus one's gaze on a circumstance or person as though that were the first cause of one's suffering; that way lie bitterness and burning resentment. Perhaps the only thing even more demoralizing is for the soul to feel it has been given up as a prey to some hostile and impersonal force—fate, destiny, and so on. Pity the men and women who believe that war, disaster and death are meaningless. We Christians know that suffering has a meaning. Our Father in heaven, who numbers the hairs on our head, who surrounds us with love, who is the very erosphere in which we live and breathe and have our being, He it is who permits that we suffer. No powerless God is He; no blind force, but our Father, as His Son has said we may call Him. It is a great consolation to be surrounded by love when we are suffering, even if our friends cannot cure the suffering. And it is a great source of peace to know that it is One who loves us who permits our suffering as He permitted it for His first-born Son, and for all His beloved sons and daughters through Christian history. We will not be tempted to bitterness and revolt if we remember in whose company we suffer: the Queen of Martyrs, the martyrs, the saints, the doctors, the confessors and the whole court of heaven. We should not regret our resemblance to them. This was the consolation of the saints. Too humble to admit any resemblance in virtue to the saints who had gone before them, they rejoiced that at least they bore some similarity to them in suffering.

Christ reveals to us on the cross that suffering is a consequence of sin. That does not mean that when I suffer I am necessarily being personally punished for my personal sins. Christ was not being punished for His. It means that suffering has a redemptive significance. We suffer to redeem ourselves and all of humanity with us. We have all offended the great and holy God and we must all repair this injustice. And so we suffer justly, we sinners. Only Christ and His

Mother suffer for love alone and not for the just reparation of their sins.

It is very important, however, to realize that the meaning of our suffering is not exhausted when we have said this. To suffer in just retribution for sin fully explains the suffering of the damned. It would be scandalous, however, to say the same of our suffering. We are living members of Christ's Mystical Body. Consequently, our suffering has much the same meaning as that of our Lord and Chief, our Head, our Christ: it is redemptive suffering, drawing the whole of this new humanity of Christ's towards redemption, bringing it to union with the God who is. Suffering makes us advance in union with God, now that Christ's suffering has opened the great door to God's presence. Suffering accomplishes in us an interior transformation and purification. Our suffering is, literally, *orientated,* it points somewhere. It has a dynamic thrust in a certain direction —in the direction of Christ, of God. It is not a meaningless torture. It is an open road, a road that we want above all to remain open. It is a way, a path, that leads somewhere: to union with God. It is not an empty period in our lives. It achieves something, for it gently but firmly moves us and all of needy humanity onto the path to union and away from all detours. This is why we can speak of a love of suffering without being morbid. Such a preference for the main road, the royal highway, is really a love of life in Christ.[3]

Suffering can bring joy to the Christian heart not because it is abnormal, but because the Christian is farsighted. He sees the lasting city at the end of the highway. The new

Jerusalem that he approaches, and its Master, Christ, await the Christian soul as the bridegroom does the bride.

There is another Christian meaning to suffering, and again it is Christ who reveals it to us: suffering is one of the most perfect expressions of the love of our neighbor. For Christ is like a great magnet drawing us all to Himself as one great body. As a result the sufferings of each of us can be meritorious for the redemption of the whole body. Not that our sufferings will dispense others from working at their salvation, but they may win for others the grace to do so. How many deathbed conversions are to be attributed to the sufferings of Christian mothers and fathers, to hidden nuns in contemplative and active orders, to the aged, the "useless," the suffering members of Christ? Suffering becomes also a sharing in that which most preoccupies the heart of Christ—the redemption of humanity. It becomes a co-operation with the Father in His unceasing labor, His great task, the building up of the Mystical Body of His Son. Finally, suffering is universal, for it can touch the whole Mystical Body. It is a lived prayer, a lived reparation for all of Christ's Body without exception. And it goes straight to the heart of the Father whose action knows no limit in space or in time.

Thus we follow the example of Christ and the way He chose to effect our salvation and our sanctification. Clearly, then, one cannot conceive of a perfect Christian life if the sign of the cross is absent. Generally speaking, the more one suffers the more he tends to perfection, provided that charity keeps pace with suffering. However, one should not attempt to measure the charity of a Christian life by the amount of suffering materially borne by that Christian. Lesser sufferings, borne with greater charity, could make a person more perfect than greater sufferings borne less perfectly. But every soul that comes to real sanctity must have some share in the cross of Christ. If a soul bears great suffering with patience and conformity to the will of God, it is reasonable to judge that the supporting motive of his patience is an intense charity and a close conformation to Christ Crucified.

THE OLD ADAM AND THE NEW

The problem of suffering must be inserted into the historical context of God's interventions in the human drama. One cannot frame this question from the purely philosophical aspect without any regard to sacred history. For we must remember that in the original plan of God, suffering had no role whatsoever in human life; it is the result of a tragic opposition of Adam's human will to the original design of God. The plan of God set in motion at creation failed through a human failure. But we have been restored in Christ, the firstborn from among the dead, who holds the primacy of all things, in whom dwells the fullness of divinity. God has foreseen in Christ all created things and all of them are ordained to Him; He is above and before all of them, and the principle of their subsistence. It is within the framework of the Incarnation, the union of humanity with its God, that one must place the problem of suffering. After the redemption, St. Paul will still speak of death, the ultimate suffering, as the last enemy which Christ must conquer in humanity. The redemption will not be fulfilled until the whole Christ has come to the term of glory; then death and suffering will be banished.

What we ought to recall, then, is that the state of sinful humanity after Adam is a state which issued from a fall. It is not the "normal" and original state of affairs. The natural state of affairs for Christ is the glory of the resurrection. In the new economy, as head of His people, Christ finds Himself in His most natural condition, not at the cross but at the resurrection. Christ's normal condition is glorious, and if this be true of Him, we see that this is the normal and natural term of the Christian people also. The purpose of the redemption is to restore man to a higher state than even the primitive one of Adam. Christ recapitulates all humanity in Himself, and through His entrance into humanity brings it to a state higher than that of unfallen Adam, *in spe*, in hope. In the divine economy humanity is entirely ordained to Christ, not to Adam. Christ comes first in the divine order of intention. Adam in Paradise was only a sketch of the glorious Second Adam. We must not, then, consider the primitive condition of Adam, felicitous though it must have been, as the definitive state of humanity. Adam's condition in Paradise was only a prelude of the glory the Christian is destined for at the Parousia, the resurrection of the total Christ.[4]

Within this framework of Christian anthropology, suffering finds its meaning. In the primitive economy neither suffering nor death existed. Originally man had been created to the image of God, and the Divine Logos transfigured the soul of Adam with a grace which made it similar to the Logos Himself. Adam was granted a share in the divine nature probably at the same moment that God breathed human life into him. At that moment he received the gift of impassibility. Immune from suffering and death, he was destined to a life of joyous intimacy with God. The Greek Fathers stress very strongly the fact that incorruptibility and immortality are a proper note of the Divine Essence Itself. To share in this incorruptibility, then, is to share in something properly divine. Since Adam participated in God's incorruptibility through the gift of the spirit, his whole self, body and soul, was penetrated by this divine freedom. The Greek Fathers also stress this incorruptibility as the primary note of sanctification. They include in it, of course, the entire notion of the divine resemblance, the divine image, the sharing in the divine nature. God communicates His life to Adam by breathing into him His spirit and thus makes him share in His own immortality and impassibility. The eternal Logos, then, the first and perfect Image of the Father, shares His own divine life with the creature, and thus the body itself is withdrawn from all death, all corruption.

It was through sin that Adam separated himself from God and lost that incorruptibility and impassibility. The sin of Adam progressively invaded the entire human race, bringing with it its tragic consequences: suffering and death. In God it is the uncreated nature of His existence on which rest His immortality and incorruptibility. But the nature of man, unlike that of God, tends to return to the nothingness from which it came. Hence, corruption, suffering, death are natural to the creature; and in those deprived of the vivifying image of God, the moral and physical corruptibility natural to them returns. The Oriental Church has always regarded death primarily as sin, spiritual death, which brings with it corporeal corruption. It is sin which draws the soul towards corporeal death, reawakening in us our natural passibility and pointing us toward physical corruption and death. Evil, in its primary sense, is sin. This is the one evil which can nowise be considered good or referred to the divine good, for it is a deprivation of the total good, which is God. Death and suffering, however, the punishments for this evil, can be looked on as referable to a superior good from the moment that we disassociate them from sin.

In the thought of the Fathers, since death and suffering are consequences of sin, they can be destroyed only with the destruction of sin itself and can be assumed into the order of redemption only when sin has first been conquered by the Redeemer.[6]

It is the union of the Word of God with our humanity which makes it possible to destroy suffering and death. The incorruptibility proper to the Son of God is communicated to His own holy Humanity as a permanent gift of the Spirit. At the moment of the Incarnation Christ planted within human nature as a whole the seed of His own proper incorruptibility. The Eternal Word of God is the source of all of Christ's human existence, causing it to share His holiness and incorruptibility. Christ, the Second Adam, assures to all humanity, through His substantial union with His own human nature, a permanent source of divine gifts. The redemption is thus a new creation: humanity is lifted to a condition higher than that which it possessed in Adam before the fall, because within it, in a permanent manner, divinity has been joined to a particular human nature, Christ's. The redemption is a restoration, for it restores man to Adam's primitive state of grace. But it is even more, for in so restoring man, God has exalted human nature by giving us this new Adam who subsists within humanity, personally united with a human nature.

The Oriental Church strongly stresses the unity of all mankind in Christ, almost to the point of making mankind one single substance with Him. The Platonism of the Greek Fathers so fully influenced their concept of unity that at times they nearly appear to say that the redemption of mankind has been accomplished at the Incarnation. We realize today that mankind is one *specific* nature with Christ, but each man's humanity is numerically different from Christ's. Nevertheless, the Greek Fathers had marvelous intuition into the unity of the whole Christ. If their realism goes somewhat too far, it does accent the unity of the Christian in Christ.

It is this "consubstantiality" of all humanity in the Lord which is at the basis of the solidarity binding us to the Divine Word. His actions are mysteriously communicated to us and benefit us because we are all united in His Mystical Body, the Church. His Body has had communicated to it, since the resurrection, the incorruptibility and the impassibility of the Eternal Word. Consequently, our bodies, united to Him through the gifts of grace, will share in this mystery of impassibility. The mysteries of Christ, His actions, have become permanent actions appropriated by humanity, naturalized within it. Since the normal and natural state of Christ's humanity, because of the grace of union, is the state of glory, it follows that our normal term as Christians will be impassibility and freedom from suffering. In the glory which radiates from Christ and which He possessed from the beginning of the world in the bosom of the Father, we Christians, too, shall know freedom from death, suffering and illness. As the Greek Fathers do not hesitate to explain, the Eternal Word of God has become man in order that we might be divinized. He shares his divine sonship with us, so that we are called and are, in very truth, adopted Sons of God. Through sanctifying grace we are sons within the Son, sharing His grace and destined to share His glory. The Word of God vivifies all of redeemed humanity. Now the heavenly Adam, Christ, has already definitely conquered sin together with its consequences: death, corruption and suffering. In principle, then, we are already liberated from these ills.[6]

The connatural state of the man, Christ, the Son of God, is the state of heavenly glory. The very humanity of Christ possessed, from the beginning of His existence, the beatific vision, and no other state could have been natural and normal for a humanity which is the humanity of God Himself. Because we share in His Sonship, this same glory properly befits redeemed humanity after the resurrection. While He lived on earth, the condition of Christ was always at once that of a *viator*, a traveller, and a *comprehensor*, one who had arrived. He experienced the fatigue, suffering and death that our humanity experiences. In this sense He was like us a traveller on the road to glory. But from the beginning of His existence as man the Word of

God dwelt also in inaccessible light, possessing within His Sacred Humanity the vision of God Himself. It could not have been otherwise. It was only in virtue of a divine decree which made Him a Redeemer that Christ was enabled to suffer at all. Now that His function of redeeming mankind has been accomplished by the Incarnation and the cross, Christ has returned to His state of glory. We should not envision this, however, as a Platonic escape from the jaws of death, or as a victory in which He abandons His flesh and His humanity. Christ remains always essentially what He is constituted by the Incarnation: the Mediator, the Redeemer, the Man-God. In Him we have had restored to us, *virtually,* the incorruptibility that flows normally from the divine nature itself.

Although we were radically redeemed at the moment of the Incarnation itself, Christ proceeded with a divine impatience, following the mandate of His Father, to His dolorous passion and death. He makes it evident that His love for the Father is unlimited, and the Father's love for the sinner is unlimited. The Father, having sent His Son with a flesh like unto our own, condemned sin in the flesh, and Christ took upon Himself the condition of slave, humiliating Himself and becoming obedient even unto the death of the cross. The world may now well know that Christ has loved the Father and that the Father has loved this world, since He sent His only Son into it that the world might not perish, but might share His eternal and incorruptible life. Christ was not sent for our condemnation but for our salvation. Before we had loved God He loved us and constituted His Son a propitiation for our sins.

It would be naive to imagine that redemption by the cross implies disagreement among the persons of the Trinity. We must avoid all rhetorical exaggeration which suggests that the Eternal Father heaped His "vengeance" and His "hatred" upon the sinless Christ. We must reject all those gross theories of substitution which imply that the innocent is punished for the guilty. And we must abandon above all any idea that Christ became guilty of sin. It is true that St. Paul uses the expression "Christ became sin" to bring home to us the fundamental identity of our sinful humanity with the sinless flesh of Christ. But neither the agony in the garden nor the desolation on the cross must be interpreted as though the soul of Christ lost the beatific vision. It is always the entire Trinity, the Son included, who planned our redemption. Only the Son became Incarnate, but the entire Trinity accomplished the Incarnation in Him.

THE TRIUMPH OF CHRIST

By the plan of God, Satan's design for pursuing humanity to death is defeated. Our Lord often pointed out that He was in conflict with an adversary, and that two great forces are organized in this world, that of Satan and that of Christ. Christ was aware that the battle would be waged upon His own body and that the victory He would gain would redound to our benefit. In His public life there are numerous passages testifying to His consciousness of an adversary of humanity. At times He challenges Satan to open conflict and drives him forth from those bodies which he had possessed. At times Satan is visualized as the organizing power behind physical and mental distress. This sense of conflict is ever present with Christ. He is aware that He has come to act within human history and to reorientate it through conquest of a spiritual power.

Jesus speaks of Satan as one with whom He must do battle and, while conscious that the victory will be His, He is also aware that the conflict will last His earthly life and end with apparent defeat. For Satan does not easily abandon his attack on humanity. From the first temptations in the desert, when he suggests to Christ that He distort His Messianic purpose, he comes again and again to act through human powers as the enemy of our human nature. There exists a spiritual force bent upon the overthrow of the divine order for the redemption of humanity. At the close of Christ's life, we hear repeated references to this power. Christ warns Simon that Satan has longed to sift him as wheat. He acknowledges the striking of Satan's hour, but adds that the devil has no power over the sinless Christ. The destruction of the world of values and the kingdom of grace together with the death of humanity: this was the victory Satan planned.

As Christ is the climax of human history, so He is also in a certain sense its intensification, its fullest density; it concentrates in Him, and the decision rests in Him. This is a hand-to-hand struggle. The first victory of Satan in the Garden of Gethsemane does not persuade Jesus to give up the contest. He arises from the agony strengthened to do battle. Christ is no superficial optimist; He is aware of Satan's power, his organizing genius, his ability to use human motives, forces, organizations. In this spirit Christ goes to the sacrifice of the cross. It is within the fragile humanity of Christ that Satan intends to obtain his victory. The antagonist met Him at the beginning of His public life and was rebuffed. But he continued to attempt the death of Christ and to work towards the ruin of men, the members of Christ.

Opposed to Christ, sin and Satan receive concrete manifestation, and they celebrate victory on the cross. The entire destructive force of sin is unveiled at the moment that Christ is handed over to its power. It appears in the garden and on the cross as though sin had obtained its ultimate intention, deicide, and as though the heavenly Adam were overthrown. But Satan overreached himself. Precisely at this point the plan of God crosses with the plan of Satan and annihilates in a dazzling victory the intentions of the adversary of our human nature. Christ takes upon Himself to expiate the sins of the entire world. He will offer, from within the heart of humanity, an act of infinite love of God, and at this moment sin is destroyed in principle. Sin, which had drawn us towards nothingness, the privation of God's incorruptible life, is now adequately expiated by the love of Christ witnessed to in His sacrificial death. The entire Trinity, Father, Son, and Holy Spirit, receive this sacrifice of love offered by a man who is also God. God has infinite honor and love restored to Him by humanity. As sin is destroyed in principle, so, too, at this same moment, the consequences of sin, suffering and death, are destroyed. Christ suffers in the name of all humanity, expiating our sins and the sins of all humanity. He went to His death on the cross, and we have gone with Him, united to Him in His redemptive intentions. Consequently we will also rise with Him. He suffers as the Head, the Chief, the Man, as all humanity, precontained in its first cell. In so suffering He redeems us all.

This is the moment when suffering and death are transformed in the Christian perspective. In presenting to the Eternal Father His death as a sublime sacrifice for the entire world, Christ makes adequate reparation for sin. Death has lost its victory over humanity; suffering has lost its venom as punishment and is now disassociated from sin; it is no longer under the primal curse. The Christian's suffering takes on this completely new aspect now that it is inserted into the history of the redemption. The Christian here below is already risen with the glorious Christ. He has already become a citizen of the celestial city. It is only proper, then, that he think the thoughts of heaven, that his conversation be in heaven. Although his body is still mortal and still delivered over to the sufferings that plague humanity, it is incorporated into Christ, and has applied to it sacramentally at Baptism the redemptive sufferings, passion and death of Christ. At Baptism the Christian is plunged into death and the resurrection of Christ. Christ's death is communicated to him almost as if he personally had suffered and died for his sins.

THE TRIUMPH OF THE CHRISTIAN

Because of our incorporation with Christ we must continue to live the passion of Christ in ourselves with a meaning and a significance. Our sufferings now lead to the same glorious toil and resurrection to which His have led. We have put on the image of the heavenly Christ in resurrection, and we continue to share His passion so that the consequences of sin die in us slowly, progressively. We are delivered over each day unto death, and the multiple sufferings of life are all only preparations for sharing in the redemptive death of Christ.

Too often death is viewed by Christians as though it were something other than a victory. Yet theology teaches us that death for the Christian is a victorious participation in the mystery of Christ's victorious death. We die in imitation of Him, and we rise to the same glorious resurrection to which He arose. When the Innocent One died, death, like suffering, had lifted from it the primal malediction issued in the Garden of Paradise. Christian death is a consequence of sin, but at the same time it is a victory, an imitation of the victory of Christ. It is with full assurance of victory that the Christian proceeds to his death, accepting this trial as a necessary condition for the fulfillment of his share in Christ's resurrection. Death is now simply a condition for our resurrection and the Parousia. Although reborn at Baptism, our mortal body still tends to corruptibility. Not until the final victory of the total Christ will we personally experience all the effects of Christ's triumph. Until then, Christ continues to suffer in us and we make up, in a mysterious fashion, the sufferings that are wanting to His passion. We join our sacrificial sufferings to the supreme sacrifice of Christ on Calvary and from this union derive a new meaning for our own suffering. This does not mean that we suffer merely in imitation of Christ's passion. We are realistically incorporated into His passion in our sufferings. The gestures of Christ in His passion become really present to us; we are really united to them.

It is quite impossible for us to grasp the value of suffering if we do not realize its function in liberating humanity. To believe that Christ substituted for us so that we would have no further need for redemption is to believe that Christ had a very low idea of humanity. What Christ did was unite Himself to us and carry us with Him to the passion and death. His redemption was so perfect that it extends to the roots of humanity and lends to man's liberty the power to co-operate with it. We are enabled to co-redeem ourselves, with Christ. By suffering and death we destroy the remains of sin within us. The great suffering of the Christian in this life is the suffering that he experiences in realizing that he has sinned. Yet, many of life's sufferings are the result not of personal sins but of original sin. In this, the Christian accepts his union with Christ and joins his daily trials with Christ's expiation, conscious that suffering now has the function of freeing humanity from sin. It is a redemptive suffering, for suffering purifies the sinner and enables him to win back his fundamental spiritual liberty. It puts him on guard against sin in the future. The sinner crucifies within his own flesh his passions and lusts: the suffering which accompanies this crucifixion is an ascetical training.

It will always be true of the Christian that this world will bring him suffering. If the world hates us, we know that it has hated Christ before us. If we were of this world, the world would love its own, but because we are not of this world, the world hates us. It is quite normal that the

Christian in the world should suffer the same fate that Christ knew: injustice, misunderstanding and persecution may often be his lot, as they were Christ's.

Satan, having lost the victory over humanity in the person of Christ, does not cease to attack humanity in us. If the world is in a certain sense under his power until the Parousia, he continues to attempt to regain a lost victory over humanity. But we who have been withdrawn from the empire of darkness and transposed into the kingdom of God's beloved Son know that the victory of Satan is temporary and illusory. With Christ we enter the battle for the whole of contemporary humanity. There will be moments when, like Christ, we will experience apparent and temporary defeat. But because of our mystical identification with Christ Crucified our sufferings are joined with His and are made redemptive. If we bear in our bodies the marks of the Lord Jesus, it is because we shall also bear the resemblance of His glory in heaven. Christianity thus has the power to lend a meaning and significance to suffering beyond our personal lives. Suffering is no longer sterile. It is no longer unintelligible. It has received its explanation in the mystical union of the Christian with Christ Crucified and the Christian's continuation of His redemptive passion. It is directed not only towards our own salvation, but, animated by charity, is meritorious and satisfactory for the members of Christ's Mystical Body at all times and places. Because we are all united in the one great communion of the Church our suffering can reach out to the most distant corners of the world to reunite humanity in its Leader.

Chapter 4

THE HUMILITY OF CHRIST

4

The Humility of Christ

Jesus has placed the virtue of humility in an entirely unique light. He has made it, as it were, His virtue. He has laid special claim to it. He has invited His disciples to learn of Him, for He is "meek and humble of heart." If Jesus has placed humility in such light, it is because humility is undoubtedly central to the Christian life. Not that humility has the inner importance of charity, for charity is a divine virtue embodying the inmost substance of all holiness, but humility is indispensable as the necessary presupposition for all other virtues. Just as pride is the fountainhead of all other sins, humility is the fountainhead of all those virtues that specifically affect our human situation. There is no possibility of understanding the Christ if we do not comprehend this great but difficult virtue of humility.[1]

The Christian virtue of humility is a reversal of all previously held standards of human greatness. The resplendent figure of Christ mocked and Christ suffering so totally upsets our idea of man that philosophers and even theologians are almost at a loss to render the idea of man intelligible in a Christian framework.

It is evident that Christ had a new concept of the dignity and greatness of man. That concept, based on Christian humility, is not easy to accept. In fact, a large portion of humanity has rejected it as unworthy of the idea of man. Even among Christians one often discerns this subconscious rejection of Christ's idea of man and of human greatness. Hence we must try to penetrate deeply into His thought on the matter. For we cannot be satisfied with a merely blind loyalty to the Christian tradition but must be Christians by intelligent conviction. To be such requires that we grasp the essence of this new conception of man. That essence is Christian humility.

THE MEASURE OF MAN

By His humility Jesus radically altered pagan ideas of what constitutes human greatness. If we examine the heroes and the wise men of antiquity, we find that they were all dominated by one concept: man is great when he is deserving and possesses *laus, gloria,* praise, glory. Glory is the measure applied to everything—even to death, for if a man dies for glory, and in a glorious fashion, all is well. Whoever does not seek glory is mean-souled, opposed to that magnanimous attitude which represented the ideal of pagan humanity. Anything less than this is for slaves and is fitting only for slaves.

What an effort it would require for the men who represent the wisdom of antiquity to behold the humble Christ and to find there any greatness. He begins His life quietly, a descendant of an ancient but subjugated race that has lost all political power and is captive to a hated people. Unlike the many false messiahs of Galilee, He evinces no desire to restore that vanished greatness. His friends are in no way conspicuous for their splendid intellects or even for their personal gifts. His teachings appeal, it seems, primarily to the uneducated. They leave the theologians of His own country unmoved, and even His relatives suspect that He has gone mad. When He announces the mystery of the Eucharist they reject Him, as one who suffers from delusions. And He ends up ridiculed and despised, one of three criminals condemned to the cross.

What an enormous transformation of our idea of man has been effected by this figure of Christ! We behold His face spat upon, and all our previous certainties desert us.[2] Is this the vocation of man? Is this the part of wisdom? Is this the ideal of human greatness? Many of us, looking at that face, walk no more with Him. Many of us, accustomed since childhood to this figure of Christ, no longer reflect on its meaning, preferring not to see that the substantial Revelation of God is still mocked and spat upon. But Christ is truly revealing a new meaning to man, the Christ-Idea of human greatness. He is issuing a call to all humanity to reconsider its nature, its vocation, and its ideal. He is defining anew the meaning of man, and if He is the Word uttered by God, He has revealed here the God-idea of humanity.

If this is to be the Christian way of life, then we must squarely face the fact that the Christian is called upon to be a contradiction to the world's idea of greatness. Our task then is to look at the mocked Christ and to ask Him what message He bears to us from God. It is certain that the God of whom He speaks cannot be merely the Supreme Being of the Philosopher. We do not expect to find the Supreme Being with spittle on his face. It is equally certain that the God of whom this figure speaks is not the god of Olympus with his cool superiority and exquisite detachment from human woes. As a matter of fact He does not fit in with any of our human ideas. Instead He is an existence plunged in unutterable mystery, a God who suffers crucifixion.

We are so used to the ultimate Christian fact of Christ Crucified that we no longer see it for what it actually is—a reversal of all past ideas of human greatness and a totally new idea of human vocation. It is possible, of course, to sentimentalize the fact, but only if we forget that this position on the cross was chosen by infinite power, and that all this long passion has no detail not willed by Freedom Itself. If we could only escape the idea that this was chosen by God as the best, life would be very much more comfortable. But the free choice of Christ stands there blocking the way to a life that would unite Christianity and a purely human idea of greatness. If we could even persuade ourselves that at this moment, at least, Christ ceased to be the great revealer, we might not have to believe that more than ever at this moment He reveals God's idea of what is good for man. If we could convince ourselves that this ignoble and unjust fate is His alone, that He went through this grinding humiliation in order that we might not go through it, then perhaps the soul could find occasion for tears of sympathy. But it seems rather that what He went through in His passion is meant for us also. It seems that an invitation issues from this figure not to weep for Him but to join Him. It seems, in short, that the life He plans for His Christians is a Christian life, almost the same type of life He led. He did not substitute Himself for us entirely. He was not mocked that we might be honored. He was not poor that we might be rich. He was not laughed at that we might be lauded. On the contrary, He was revealing what we may call "a Christian picture of man," one that was meant to include us too. Consequently we can no longer project upon God our human ideas of what He should be like but, reversing the process, we must learn what man should be from what God was like on earth.

In entering human history God has shattered all previous conceptions of what God is and what man should be. He has revealed Himself as Love. He has revealed that in imitation of Him we are called to be great only in humility and in love. We bow before this mystery of God mocked, condemned, suffering. We accept the greatness of humility and the evidence that we must grow as humans only by humility. "He must increase, I must decrease." The spirit naturally trembles before the perspectives of this new philosophy of life. Nevertheless, we who have been so careful of the respect due to us must learn to accept contempt with more than equanimity. We must learn to respect it. We can no longer glory in our intelligence or in our learning, in our efficiency or in our accomplishments.

All complacency must disappear before the sight of everlasting Wisdom freely choosing contempt. The yearning for recognition and the restless eagerness to "get ahead" no longer have a meaning for the Christian. The soul filled with restless ambition seems to be filled with a consuming fire, but it is not the fire of Christian charity. Christian love takes another direction entirely: "*ama nesciri et reputari nihilo*"—"love to be unknown and considered as nothing." All other things being equal, to prefer contempt to honor, to prefer ridicule to praise, to prefer humiliation to glory—these are some of the classic Christian formulas for greatness. To accept failure, having done our best; to welcome insults and rebukes; to long for the last place and the least dignity: this is the ultimate core of Christian humility, and this is the Christian ideal of greatness. It is an ideal possible to all, and it is an ideal that grows less strange the more we practice it, for humility gradually reveals its inner suavity and beauty to the soul that strives to obtain it. What at first sight seems unnatural and inhuman reveals with familiarity the true greatness it contains and fosters. And the face of Christ is nowhere more Godlike than when it is the face of Christ mocked and suffering.

After the descent of the Holy Ghost upon the apostles, they who had longed for human glory and for human greatness learned the lesson of the new humanity Christ had come to create. "And they left the presence of the Council, rejoicing that they had been found worthy to suffer indignity for the sake of Jesus' name." This is a perfect example of the reversal of values to which Christ calls us. "God forbid that I should make a display of anything, except the cross of our Lord Jesus Christ, through which the world stands crucified to me, and I to the world. . . .

is impossible for man to orientate himself towards God until this fundamental selfishness is eradicated by Baptism. Even then the effects of original sin exist within him always as a seed of possible revolt. In order to reorientate himself to God he needs humility. As a creature, man cannot have happiness from himself but only as received. His happiness is always a participated glory, and when the soul seeks unparticipated glory, glory from itself alone, it commits implicit blasphemy, setting itself up in the place of the absolute and taking what is proper to God alone.[3]

Humility is a virtue which gives us a realistic idea of the low place which belongs to us, and St. Paul always treats it as the condition necessary that charity may flourish. St. John too stresses the need of this virtue for the man approaching faith. No one can come to Christ unless the Father has drawn him, but the great obstacle to the Father's drawing is self-love, love of human glory. This is why man refuses the offer of God's love in Christ. Setting himself up as his own end, man eventually turns to a quasi-idolatry of self in radical opposition to God. It is possible for him to love God disinterestedly, but only at the price of painful renunciation and humility. In this sense man's love is quite different from the effortless love of God. Christ came to assume our human nature, which had fallen under the dominion of sin, and to heal our whole existence. Like to us in all things save the guilt of sin, He came in total unselfishness to teach us to die to that false self-love which militates against divine life. In His death on the cross Christ accomplished for us this mystery of death to self.

It is worthy of note that Christ presents His passion and

death as something which "ought to be," a condition for the glorification of His body. The same holds true for the disciple.

As humility is a necessary condition for glory, it is also a necessary condition for fraternal charity. We know from the beginning of our Christian training that the cross of Christ is the supreme symbol of God's love for men. He came to give His life as a ransom for many, and greater love than this no man hath. Yet the disciple is called upon to imitate Him in serving and, if necessary, in giving his life for the brethren. Sacrifice and humiliation are often a proof of one's love for the Church.

In Pauline theology, the close connection between sacrifice and love is brought out very clearly. When Christ comes to humanity He finds it in a fallen state; to lift it to grace He must perform that total act of self-giving which was His death. If He is to pass definitively with His humanity to a state where God is His total life, He must pass through the effect of sin, which is death, until He destroys its power and it no longer has dominion over Him. His passion is His passage to God, to a wholly divine life. By it Christ receives in His human nature that glorification which belongs to Him as the proper Son of God. The glory of His divinity is manifested permanently, definitively, in His humanity only after He has withdrawn from the influence of the effects of sin. It is the resurrection of Christ, the completion of the passion, which puts the final seal of redemption upon man. At that moment Christ exercises most fully His salvific will. It is then that He begins to live the life where God is the total form of His human existence.

We must recall that Christ became man not for His sake but for ours; He rose for our justification. The passion of Christ, as we have seen, is the means by which we pass from sin to the life of God, and it must be applied to us in order that we may share in His glory. We also pass through the same Pasch which He passed through, gradually realizing within ourselves the mystery of the cross and the resurrection. This process of the spiritualization of humanity began on the day of the Lord's resurrection and will continue until the second coming of Christ. Our holiness is therefore a progressive immersion in the double mystery of Christ's death and resurrection.[4] As St. Thomas Aquinas teaches, the sacraments apply Christ's passion to us. Penance reforms our disorientation and the Eucharist conforms us to Christ, applying to us the paschal mystery and continuing Christ's gestures in time. Hence the Christian must continually renounce himself, accepting suffering and humiliation as the true way to grow in Christ.

HUMILITY AND TRUST

At times one encounters misleading and dangerous misconceptions of this Christian virtue of humility. Humility, like every other virtue, is parodied by a pseudo-virtue which imitates it in a distorted fashion and without the inner power which real virtue has for man's fulfillment. There are Christians who think they are humble because they engage in a sort of self-hating, tormenting conflict which destroys their psychical balance. But real humility, while acknowledging our nothingness before God, is always balanced by the firm confidence that He intends to save us and that He is omnipotent. The Christian at times speaks of himself as worthless, depreciating his value before God. This is correct inasmuch as all we have of ourselves is worthlessness and sinfulness, but we balance this conviction with the realization that God has acted within us and that His gifts are not to be despised. The ancients said that the gods hated *hubris,* overweening pride, but loved *sophrosune,* that moderation and prudence which the older spiritual writers call *discretio.* Humility, therefore, requires neither lacerating self-criticism nor compulsive self-depreciation. Behind this sort of self-condemnation lurks *hubris.* The man given over to such a temptation longs in his heart for the absolute goodness of God. He seeks to appropriate moral perfection and to wear it as a decoration but without the inner value that it possesses in the sight of God. And always in this compulsive, self-destructive criticism there is a certain rigid refusal to accept one's small stature before God. An irrational anger at one's own failures poisons the mind. What else should we expect of ourselves, save failure, fault and defects?

It is a good thing, however, for a man to recognize the limitations of his nature and not to ascribe to his freedom a totality and unconditioned quality that it does not possess. We must be patient with ourselves as God is patient with us, and strive quietly, consistently and without interior torment to reach the high goals which God has placed before us. To reach these goals the divine assistance is required and given. One cannot, by whipping oneself to a frenzy, attain an iota more of grace. For grace is always a divine gift. The face of Christian humility reflects an interior peace.

Those who, disclaiming "mediocrity," make their motto "all or nothing" are gravely deceived. Although we must constantly try to grow in generosity, we must always remember that something is better than nothing. To refuse this something is to arrogate to oneself an angelic nature rather than to accept the human nature which God has chosen to give us. We make progress by definite steps, and it is not a sign of Christian virtue to insist upon immediate possession of absolute holiness. Instead, we should be content with the acknowledgement that we are sinful and capable of every sin if God's grace were withdrawn.

But it is not necessary or even desirable to insist that we are the worst of men. Generally speaking, such statements should be left to the saints, who have received inner lights from God, making them aware of their own sinfulness. And even when these statements are uttered by the saints they do not imply that the saints actually consider themselves worthless. They simply mean what we can all say in truth: that we have nothing of value that has not been given to us by God. The saint who stresses that he is the most ignoble, worthless and most sinful of men could also truthfully sing the Magnificat: "He that is mighty has done great things in me." For Christian virtue is usually a complex thing. Meekness, for example, unites in itself qualities which might seem opposed to its very nature; it is powerful, strong, bold, resourceful and enduring. In the same way, Christian humility is tranquil, confident and courageous. The coercive demands which some Christians make upon themselves and their overemphatic, hysterical self-condemnation do not reveal a Christian virtue but a psychological deficiency which humility might well cure. Although grace is not ordinarily given to operate clinical cures, the person who possesses humility manifests healthy equilibrium in all his judgments concerning himself.

THE PHARISAIC TEMPTATION

Christ has also warned the Christian to be particularly on his guard against any form of self-righteousness.[5] Self-righteousness, in fact, is in direct opposition to the spirit which breathes from the Gospels, for it depreciates the mystery of God. Christian morality, the most interiorized morality ever proposed to man, insists very strongly upon the gift-character of all moral progress. We are transformed by the action of Another, and it is our human task freely to accept this activity of God. But the man who glorifies self regards morality as a means of self-satisfaction. This is contrary to the very spirit of morality. The man who seeks to satisfy his pride by fulfilling the letter of the law, while avoiding its inner spirit, directly attacks the absolute moral sovereignty of God. The falseness of such an attitude is realized most fully in those who make use of their obedience to prescribed law as the reason for accounting themselves just while condemning their neighbor.

There is an inflexible hardness which characterizes the self-sufficient man. His inhuman coldness uses morality itself as a weapon against the sinner. This is a far cry from the Christian way, which is characterized by the imitation of the God of Love. But the rationality of the self-sufficient man reveals, when analyzed, a terrifying absence of charity. Rejoicing in what he considers to be his own moral superiority, the self-righteous man seems almost to rejoice in the moral failures of others. He does not merely compare himself favorably to others; he actually seems to enjoy the defects of others since these satisfy his own feeling of superiority. Flattering himself that he is not like the rest of men, the man of proud moral correctness and pseudo-justice strikes directly at the heart of Christian life. This is the reason why Christ so insistently castigated the Pharisees. Humility is the basic condition for the flowering of all Christian virtue.[6]

The ambiguous situation of the stony-hearted man is revealed in action. Selecting from the moral order those things which can most easily be formulated juridically, he abandons all other precepts, including the major one of loving God, and he appears unaware that a deep-going contempt of others is of its nature always a mortal sin. Instrumentalizing the highest of moral values, he attains his end by despising the rest of men, again apparently unaware that he has voided all his own morality. What is particularly repugnant about such a Christian is that he invokes the power and the name of God as weapons against his neighbor. But this is death to the spirit of Christian meekness, mercy and charity.

The coldness, rigidity and rationality of the Pharisee's judgment of others amazes us by its destructive power. The Pharisee actually despises mercy; refusing to appeal to God's mercy himself, he is irritated that God is merciful to the sinner. Arrogating to himself the position of judge, he finds even God wanting for daring to exercise His mercy. Lacking all sense of solidarity with the sinner, he experiences only revulsion in his presence. In the hands of Pharisaic Christians, Christianity often seems no more than a well-organized social form which endorses respectability in bourgeois society.

This type of man, when confronted with a genuine Christian attitude of humility, charity or mercy, finds himself in complete opposition. He will at times describe such Christian virtues as exaggerated, mystical, irrational or in bad taste, whereas in fact his own type of loveless morality is purely formal in its submission to God. For when the appeal of God is issued in a special situation not clearly defined by law, a man of this type normally feels no responsibility to engage himself at any personal risk. Without humility, he sits in judgment upon his fellow men, relishing his own supposed moral superiority, unrealistically blind to his utter dependence upon the goodness of Another.

Chapter 5

HOPE AND FEAR

5

Hope and Fear

Perhaps the most difficult of the virtues to comprehend is hope. Hope sometimes appears, in the usual description of it, less a virtue than a sort of spiritual selfishness focussing our attention exclusively upon ourselves and the reward due us, as we hope for our salvation from God together with the means to obtain it. But this is not a true description of hope.

HOPE IN THE OLD TESTAMENT

The virtue of hope is essentially a communal virtue with an historic orientation.[1] We can realize this more fully if we reflect on God's gradual revelation concerning hope. At a certain moment in history He called to Himself Abraham, and announced to him that he would be the father of a great and divinely chosen people. God thus broke into our human conversation with a new word, a new orientation, a new direction for history. He told Abraham—and He meant the message for all men—that human life, all historic life, has a meaning, a term and a destiny. The meaning is from its term, the Savior to come. Abraham's response to this message was one of hope—a generous, ardent clinging to the promise of God. And this was wise. For no one, in fact, can live successfully in an atmosphere of hopelessness and despair. If the world in which we live seems to have no rational interpretation, no term towards which it is moving, then all the evils of life are final. All the deep seriousness of life then becomes more than seriousness: it becomes meaningless suffering and tragedy. But hope is a light placed by God in the darkness, assuring us that all reality is as so many threads in the divine hands woven toward a definite term—the coming of the Messias, the Savior.

Because this revelation had been made to him Abraham became a man of great desires, a forward-looking man. Because of this revelation he was renewed in vigor, for he knew that he was part of the great movement towards the term. In the years that intervened between Abraham and the coming of Christ, this communal hope of Abraham's people, of all nations, was kept alive through history. One may even say that the history of the human race before Christ is a history of the virtue of hope. The purpose of all existence is defined for the Jewish people by the moment in which their Savior will install in their midst the long awaited kingdom of God.[2]

The Old Testament notion of hope is always communal. For many centuries of Old Testament times the question of individual reward or retribution is not even raised, and when finally it is asked, the answer is vague and unsatisfactory, precisely because it is *not* the primal question. The primal question is: What is to happen to the *laos*—the people of God? The people, the group, the whole count for much, and the individual shares in the destiny of his people. So it is, too, with Christian hope.

HOPE IN THE NEW TESTAMENT

Christ inaugurated Christian hope when He replaced the Old Testament idea of a material messianic kingdom with the notion of an eschatological kingdom, the kingdom to come at the end of the world, when the whole Church will triumph in Him and reflect the glory of the Trinity. On that day man will possess the Trinity, and the first instinct of human nature will be satisfied. He will be loved by God as a Triune Personality, and the second need of his nature will be fulfilled. The alterations that Christ has made in the work of hope are its fulfillment. He has promised the coming of the kingdom. Christian hope is still fixed upon a definite moment in time; hope still integrates the movement of this world and all its history. The individual shares in the hope of the whole Church, anticipating the triumph of the whole people of God. Christian hope is still communal, existing at the same time within each heart as a share in the Church's life.[3] It is orientated towards an event in time, the event which closes time—the second coming of Christ. It is not directed exclusively towards the moment after my death, towards *my* possession of the beatific vision. This is included in my hope for my people. But the prime object of my hope is the salvation of the whole Christ. Hope is an expectation which rests upon the love of God for the new Israel. It expects from Him the glorification of this new Israel. It expects that which exceeds all man's natural powers—the open vision of God.[4]

Christian hope is thus closely connected with charity, for we hope not only for ourselves but for all men united with us in the Church. It is a transposition of my selfish desires for happiness into the order of grace. Here Christian happiness is essentially dynamized by a second orientation of spirit. Christian happiness is both a giving and a receptivity. The object of my hope is nothing that can be annexed. It is something that I must dispose myself to receive. At the end of the Church's earthly lifetime, when God the Son delivers the Church over into the hands of His Father, we hope to be also delivered over as members of that final kingdom. We await this triumph with a confidence that empowers us to endure all the difficult things of life, for the foundation of our confidence is God Himself. We turn to Him, not only as to one who has infinite power to help us but as to one who is, as St. Thomas observes, *pius,* considerate, understanding, concerned about us. Preoccupied with the creaturedom He has made, He guides it towards its final destiny. Therefore we look to Him for the means necessary to achieve the triumph of His Church.

Our confidence is thus integrated of two attitudes: distrust of self and trust in God. As we grow older and wiser, we do not grow more confident in ourselves, but become conscious of how little we can rely upon self for the end we have in view. Even our failures, however, cause us greater hope. All our inadequacies, deficiencies, and defects, even our sins, can be integrated into this virtue of hope. They cause not bitter resentment or discouraged return upon ourselves, but rather a clear-eyed awareness of our task and of how incompetent we are to achieve that task.

But this distrust of self builds within us a greater trust in Him who has infallibly promised to give us all the means we need to attain our individual triumph within the communal triumph of the Church. For our hope is not based merely upon God's justice or fidelity, but upon His loving paternal mercy for His creature. The ultimate grace which we hope for, for ourselves and for each member of the Church, is the free and unmerited gift of final perseverance. The fact that we are dependent upon God's mercy and that our hope is anchored in that divine attribute should not diminish within us the mentality of the conqueror—for that is the mentality of the Christian—but rather remind us only that we conquer *in another.* We have only to co-operate, and even that co-operation is willed by God within us. Wholly dependent on His mercy, we live in an all-conquering trust that heaven will be ours. The spirit that dynamizes us, making difficult and arduous things seem easy because we are secured and anchored in this confidence, is the very Spirit of God.

Hope is also an unusual virtue in that it stands at the crossways of two fundamental orientations. Because man is created needy, expectant and necessarily dependent, he has within him, as Gabriel Marcel has put it, a basic tendency to *have* things. He tends to acquire possessions, to render things his, extending his personality and prolonging himself in all he can dominate. This is a permanent impulse of the human heart, for man is needy. He needs things to grow and to subsist. Yet within his spirit man encounters another God-given impulse flowing from his nature as spirit. Spirit can grow and develop only by transcending itself, by giving itself away. The primal need of spirit is to love and to be loved: to enter into communion. This it does, not by acquiring, possessing, annexing, but by self-giving.[5]

Hope stands at the center of these two dynamic orientations of spirit and it unifies the two, for one cannot give himself away except it be in the firm, unwavering expectation that upon the giving of oneself there will flow back something that could never be annexed, but must be received as a gift of God. My soul thirsts to possess or, better still, to receive the Uncreated Goodness, God Himself. But if one spends all his life in annexing things, he becomes gradually dominated by an attitude of "having." This attitude tends to close the spirit in on itself, frustrating the other fundamental orientation to receive until to give oneself away finally appears to be unnatural. Conflict then arises within our nature. One must surpass and transcend himself; he must give himself away to fulfill himself. But this is impossible if he is dominated by the instinct to acquire and to possess. Hope now enters upon the scene, intimating to the soul that if it dares to follow the suggestion of love and give itself to God, there will flow back to it, by the law that governs giving, a good supreme above all goods, the Gift of God Himself.

From this point of view Christian hope is completely unique. It does not merely enlarge the domain of human expectations beyond this life but it directs them towards a good which surpasses man's greatest possibilities. Not only does it equip the Christian to look beyond the frontiers of this world for his peace, but it draws him to a completely new sphere of things, to an order and good which surpass, as St. Paul tells us, all human imaginings—the infinite good which is God Himself.

It is precisely for this reason that hope is at once an obligation and a gift. It is an obligation because God has commanded us to hope, and it is a gift because only through the power of God are we enabled to hope for such a good. The infused virtue of hope does not arise as a complement to any natural desire of the human will for goodness. It arises from the fact that the Christian is reborn at Baptism and equipped for a sovereignly new type of happiness, the vision of God Himself. For this happiness he is to hope, and the very capacity for hope is divinely implanted by God. Without this summons from the All-High to seek this happiness, man could have no hope for it, for it would be impossible to attain.

Hope is thus one of the three infused virtues orientating us towards the term of grace, Vision. It develops with the development of sanctifying grace in those reborn in Christ. The Christian's expectation, it is true, looks to God for assistance in all the trials of this life, but it especially looks to Him for the possession of God Himself. The Christian is aware that he must conquer the repeated temptations of self and the world and persist in seeking the object of his hope. For this he requires special graces beyond even the indwelling grace of the Holy Spirit; he needs the divine mercy bending over him the whole length of the road and maintaining him in constancy. This unchanging assistance of God, daily renewed in the soul of the baptized, is also an object of hope, since without it the final object itself could not be attained.

HOPE AND THE SINNER

What God has done, therefore, is to step into the pattern of human life and to unify all human desires by pointing out to man his genuine last desire. He has revealed to us the unity of our longing as Christians, delivering us from the distracting and fevered search for lesser goods. Thus it is that the Christian leans upon God for the special assistance needed in this life and for the great gift of final perseverance.

Even the sinner is able to persevere in this hope if he has not directly attacked by his sin the virtue of hope itself. We often observe in life the man who loves God, but not sufficiently; who prefers himself to God, but who yet abandons God with reluctance. Such a one can no longer hope in God in the same way as can a soul gifted with the energizing charity of grace. Yet it is possible that his trust in a merciful God may survive his spiritual shipwreck. For he may cling to the hope that on the last day God will mercifully bend over him and renew in him that charity he once knew. In a strange way, and one that suits the complexity of the human soul, the sinner still hopes in God even though he remains freely separated from God. It is only by direct attack upon hope itself that hope can be destroyed; only the damned need lose it. For this reason St. Paul refers to hope as the anchorage of our souls, firm and immovable, reaching that inner sanctuary beyond the veil, where Christ our escort has already entered.

There are those who, stumbling under the burden of human wretchedness, wonder if they still hope in the helping God. They begin to feel that they should despair since God seems to have forgotten them, so filled with sin are their lives. Yet even among these there is at times an attitude of hope, of waiting, trusting that the providence of God will alter the pitiful circumstances of their existence. It is only those, however, who take back from the hands of Christ their future and decide to accomplish their destiny without His help who really despair and are lost. When a man decides that God is incapable of further mercy and separates himself from the people of God, one rightly wonders about his final lot. It is not possible, of course, to plumb the depths of the soul, and at times even the worst of sinners appear to be making a faint gesture of appeal to God, which is perhaps the beginning of hope. At times too, although overcome with revulsion at his own life, the sinner summons up sufficient courage to believe that despite appearances God will not tempt him beyond his strength, and that he should cast himself upon His mercy. It may not be altogether clear how one can lean upon the helping God and still sin. Yet doubtless many look to him in some obscure fashion to help them conform to what they really desire in the depths of their being. Even they can somehow fall back upon God and put their trust in Him.[6]

The human heart has depths whch are not explored by juridical procedures.*

THE PSYCHOLOGY OF HOPE

Because of its power to arouse our energy and courage to continue the fight for all that leads to the final good, hope has an effect upon our whole world-view. By nature many of us are phlegmatic. Our temperaments are slow, heavy, resistant. Perhaps sad experience has taught us a certain distrust of the future; perhaps it has taught us that tomorrow may well bring grief and that we should be warned against too great joy today. Certain temperaments seem to be naturally pessimistic, falling back easily before the shocks of human existence. Especially if a man's life has been full of trials and disappointments, a certain listlessness and lack of resiliency may be evident in his entire approach. He may look always upon the dark side of things, regarding the future with fear and anxiety. The result is a temperament which seems altered in its vital sources. The springs of energy having worn down, the soul, weary and disillusioned, turns in upon itself, expecting only the worst from outside. In such a situation hope enters, bringing new vigor to our lives, enabling us to look to the future, not by disregarding the present but by recognizing its passing, transitory gift-character as something arranged by God. The sight of the future perfect good arouses in us an impatient energy. A stable power charges the soul, recreating desire within us, renewing contact with life, giving new strength

* For a fuller treatment of this point the reader is referred to the Appendix to this chapter, "Grace and Liberty."

for battle and a joyous foretaste of victory. Fully aware that God cannot delude us, that He invites us to the glory of His kingdom, we know that He will keep us firm in the faith until the day when we greet the coming of the Lord Jesus Christ.

Strong in faith in the divine promises, man relies upon the oath of God. For as St. Thomas points out, the New Testament *is* a testament, an inheritance willed by Christ to us, His people. God will carry on what He has begun in us in the unity of Christ. Theological hope, since it leans upon the fidelity of God Himself, possesses an inner certainty not drawn from empirical proof. Everything in the Christian life should press towards the fulfillment of that life with a certain living dynamism.

There is no doubt that the Christian is often inspired, remembering his own sinfulness and the depths he has sounded, to question not whether God will be faithful in giving but whether he himself will be faithful in receiving God's gifts. As maturity comes illusions pass, and the ordinary man becomes aware that he can lay small claim to anything like constancy in goodness. On the contrary, as he recalls his pettiness, his gropings and his falls, a certain distress and unformulated uneasiness begin to chill the heart.

But at this point the disciple of Christ turns to the unshakable foundation of his hope: God Himself, who has called him, who has created him, and who knows what has gone into his making. Therefore He will not despise the good will even of the sinner. Trusting not in his own justice but in the constancy and fidelity of God, the Christian knows that hope is the answer to the uneasiness and the distress of his personal existence. The Christian hopes because God has called upon him to do so: "May God, the author of our hope, fill you with joy and peace in your believing" (Rom. 15:13). But God is also, paradoxically, the source of fear.

FEAR IN THE OLD TESTAMENT

With the saints of the Old Testament terror in God's presence was a familiar experience. Yahweh is a devouring fire in whose presence no man may open his eyes. Isaias warns us that while we need not fear the lesser powers of this world, our proper terror should be God Himself. Daniel fell senseless in the presence of this unveiled majesty. So overpowering was the presence of God to the Old Testament saint that it almost seems as though God's demands were too exigent, striking terror into the heart of man. There was need for Yahweh to conceal the blinding radiance of His divinity under the benign humanity of Christ.

In the presence of total power, man finds it difficult to recall that this power is also total love.[7] Disturbed, anguished, conscious of his sinfulness, he recoils from closer dealings with God. One can only grasp the amazing love revealed in the New Testament when he has first understood the naked power of the jealous God of the Old Testament. Yahweh seizes upon the Hebrews and demands that they follow His ordinances. He does this with no previous invitation from them. Had He remained hidden like the gods of the pagans, their presence but suspected in natural phenomena, the Hebrew could perhaps have dealt with

Yahweh without fear. But God is not content to remain the wholly transcendent, concealed in unaccessible light. He initiates a conversation with man and lays down His exigencies. He threatens with a special terror those who disobey Him. His devouring purity insists upon purity from us. His presence reveals to man all his radical incapacity to fulfill the demands of God, except through the power of God. He menaces man with His threats to prevent his entering into the detour of sin, and the election of the Jews by no means lessened their fear of the God who had chosen them. He constantly charges them with their infidelity, their failure, their stiff-necked refusal to accept His love. The whole law and all the Prophets ceaselessly repeat the terrifying thunderings of God towards the man who abandons His path.

The devout Jew is always aware of his own past infidelity, or of the possibility in the future. This is always before him, along with the memory of those terrible curses with which God threatens the unfaithful. The Old Testament uses extremely concrete terms to express this fear of man before his God. Man trembles to the very marrow of his bones and is exposed on all sides to insecurity in this relationship. The omnipotence of God seems to crush by its presence. The naked power of divinity comes as an annihilating shock to fragile humanity. All human support is of no avail to man. We have only to think of the figure of Job before his God.[8]

The Old Testament bears witness not only to the anguish of the sinner but also to the fear of the just. This is, of course, a qualitatively different fear from that of the sinner. God permits it, but it will some day end through His providence, whereas the anguish of the sinner on this earth is a pale image of what his future will be when he falls into the hands of the living and seeing God. The anxiety of the just man has its own remedy. If he but opens his heart and expresses his anguish, God shows Himself loving and merciful. One cannot grasp the meaning of hope in the New Testament until one has experienced the spiritual climate surrounding this virtue in the Old Testament. There God orders His people to hope in His fidelity, and forbids them to give way to fear of persecution from enemies or indeed from any human power. They are to fear Him and Him alone. When they observe this command, He protects them and gives a meaning to their human sorrows, each of which is a further stage in the fulfillment of the future kingdom of Israel.

FEAR IN THE NEW TESTAMENT

The New Testament moves in quite a different atmosphere. Here again we find the natural anguish of mankind encountering the God of judgment. In the New Testament, too, the day of the Lord is a day of terror, as the Apocalypse points out, but it is also, even primarily, a day of fulfillment, an aspect which the Old Testament does not strongly accent.

The New Testament is distinguished from the Old in another point also. The New Testament gives ground for a more intense fear of the sinner than does the Old, for in the New Testament hell has had its meaning unfolded. The Gospel reveals far more about the eternal fate of the sinner than the dim and vague *sheol* of the Old Testament. When we read the Gospel descriptions of hell, we see that the anguish of the sinner has been intensified until it is almost insupportable. The visions of the Apocalypse surpass in terror anything found in the Old Testament.

In the New Testament, the terrors of the just are also intensified. Those who find themselves before God, without the intermediary of human messengers, are terrified. The disciples on Thabor, the women at the tomb, the apostles after the resurrection of Christ, Paul at the apparition of Christ: all these are struck to the heart by the immediacy of the divine. Notwithstanding, the notion of fear is considerably altered in the New Testament. While Jesus Himself seems to experience successive invasions of anguish, in the Temple before His death, in Gethsemane, on the cross, He had nevertheless completely altered the meaning and content of human fear.[9]

From the moment when Christ finally transformed fear upon the cross, our anguish, suffering and fear include within themselves a possibility of transformation. Implicit within them is a new orientation. Christianity will explore that orientation and will transmute fear into something that is secondary and encircled by joy. In the New Testament anguish will become a sort of lightsome darkness. It will be directed towards the transformation of the Church into a bride without spot or blemish. It will be pointed towards that final resurrection in which the universe will radiate the glory of its God. Its role will be to prepare us to mirror upon the face of the world the face of the eternal God. On the cross anguish was altered to its roots, for there the redemption was objectively accomplished. At that moment fear underwent an inner transformation which objectively transmutes it. But it is now also altered *subjectively* as qualitative experience, if the Christian submits to it in faith. God now demands of us a special approach to fear. We are no longer living in the Alliance of the Promise, but in the last times. We have heard the oath that God has sworn and has kept: His oath of redemption.

Paradoxically, while the Christian is not free from fear, he is nevertheless commanded by God to be free from fear. This may sound unreal, but the explanation is quite simple. He who in the night of terror holds the hand of God with strong faith, hope and charity, as he is ordered to, is conscious of a border of light surrounding his darkness. Fear, which has now a redemptive share in the agony of Christ, is never given to the man of the New Alliance without previous taste of the supporting joy of Christ Himself. There is no such thing in Christian existence as a fear that lasts during the whole of a man's life. That would be impossible. God alternates sieges of desolation and depression with delight, until the fears of man are entirely encircled with the luminous joy of the Resurrected Christ. Christ has ascended on high, taking captivity captive, and all the forces that assail man's humanity have been rendered captive to His yoke. Fear is among these forces, and although it is still able to assail humanity, it has been radically crushed. Therefore, the Christian no longer has reason for unqualified fear. He is a redeemed creature, living in a universe essentially redeemed, whose redemption he is to further. The prince of this world is no longer Satan, now vanquished by Christ. The Christian is co-conqueror in Christ's victory. The mysterious "wickedness in high places" has lost its terrors for the Christian. Christ is sovereign King of the universe, and He waits still for the fulfillment of His victory in the resurrection from the dead. He has already entered personally into the possession of the kingdom and made all humanity's enemies his footstool, including the sovereign Adversary of our human nature, Satan. The world and its powers have been disarmed by Christ, and the fear that accompanies their presence has had its venom removed. There are certainly things in this world which tend to terrorize man. But it is also true that they have lost their unintelligibility, surrounded as they are by the light that streams from the cross. Thus, the existential anguish of some modern philosophers has no role in Christianity. This is a question of faith, and when faith is weak it betrays itself in the experience of fear. While we may sympathize with those whose weakness of faith is the cause of their inner anguish, we cannot ourselves yield to such fear, for Christ has conquered it.

The world today is experiencing a crisis of nerve-racking anxiety, and the neurotic terrors that inhabit the psyche of modern man seem to increase. Nevertheless, with the bold realism of faith, the Christian casts himself upon the protecting God. This does not mean that the Christian will not experience anguish, but that he will experience it without revolt or unintelligibility, and that he will experience it between two phases of joy. Even in the experience of fear itself the entire emotional content will be anchored in an immovable confidence. For the individual in the New Testament fears "within the Church," ecclesiologically: he fears within the bosom of a body moving towards its destined term and his fears have an effect upon this body's future. He is hastening the advent of the day of the Lord. There is no such thing in Catholicism as purely private grief, purely private fear, purely private suffering. United with the whole of humanity in his fear, the Christian is no longer susceptible to the terrifying vertigo that possessed the pre-Christian world in the presence of God. Man may not always live up to the demands of his faith, but if he does, he will be liberated from fear as a final experience, knowing it only as a transitory, meaningful, redemptive emotion wholly surrounded by joy in faith.

Catholicism insists with undiminished strength on the objectivity of redemption, accomplished once and for all by Christ the Redeemer, but it insists equally that the Christian must appropriate this redemption to himself. To the extent that he does, he shares in the sufferings of the Crucified, but he shares also in the interior, social joy of the Christian co-operating in the redemption. Even the dark night of the soul is a night between radiant days, penetrated with the light of faith, operative although not directly experienced. The subjective anguish is objectively a noble work of co-redemption, a joy to the Christian in whom infused faith is the primary interpreter of existence, the lasting source of all security, the unchallenged basis upon which every supposition rests.

Appendix

GRACE AND LIBERTY

It is well here to recall what psychology teaches about the human conscience. The moral strivings of the individual do not spring from an autonomy so total that everything which appears in clear consciousness is automatically free. This is an outworn idea of human liberty, no longer able to help us in judging the responsibility of the sinner. If we believe that man is possessed of a personal conscience, and therefore is free in every situation that reaches the level of consciousness, we are dangerously close to the illusion of false independence. By such a norm people could be found guilty of all sorts of things for which in fact they are not at all responsible. The only sound morality is one in accordance with man's existential nature, which will always be valid in every concrete situation and which cannot be rejected as an illusory norm of life for some abstract, nonexistent man. Without exaggerating infra-conscious determinisms, we must clearly grasp that freedom, liberty, responsibility are not automatically to be equated with clear consciousness. Man's liberty is conditioned by many factors which precede his liberty and which he can mold, alter, and guide only indirectly. Within the limits set by these non-free conditions, man has his personal conscience to assist him in directing his spiritual life, but it would be folly to deny the play of unconscious tendencies and movements. We must not assume without proof that the conditions for moral acts are almost invariably present in the sinner. For morality man requires responsibility, liberty and an evaluation of his own action. Nor will it do simply to say that the majority of men are totally free in all their clearly conscious acts while all the rest are mad. The continuity between the normal and the abnormal state is an accepted fact in modern psychology.

There is an influence of environment and heredity upon man. We all suffer from hereditary faults. As every psychologist knows, there are many defects, ordinarily labeled moral—such as stealing, lying, selfishness, laziness—which are often the results of psychical disturbances, misdirection of will or emotions, and unconscious repressions, rather than of free moral decisions. The excessively anti-social feelings of many thieves and murderers are rarely without some quality of the psychological order which may diminish their responsibility before God. Those of excessively aggressive, domineering, quarrelsome natures, those of jealous temperaments, and those of ill-regulated emotional conduct, frequently manifest a precarious and fragile stability. Their responsibility may be limited.[10]

The freedom of man is affected too by his sociological situation. Today man thinks in sociological terms and his emotional and spiritual climate is touched by the attitudes common in the society about him. Consequently there exists today a large proportion of people in whom we cannot assume normal balance as an habitual condition. For men's judgments are influenced by opinion and the climate in which they live. Propaganda and the collective pressures exerted in the modern world tend to diminish personal liberty, moral judgment and responsibility. We begin life as a member of a community, and psychological influences are immediately exerted on us. To construct one's personality in isolation from these ties and conditions is impossible. Sociologists may tend to exaggerate the influence of the group upon the individual conscience, but the theologian has also the task of examining the conditions of liberty.

Two extremes must be avoided if we are to make any realistic judgment concerning the sinner's situation. One is the tendency to consider the conscious self as only a small segment of the person, the least important, one completely dominated by self-conscious urges. The other is to believe that the conscious is the only real personal self and that it suffers little or no influence from what lies beneath it, thus exaggerating liberty and giving the sinner a false sense of responsibility and independence. As a consequence he is sometimes forced to bear the entire burden of an unconscious life for which he could not possibly be responsible. We should not forget that there are structures existing within us (as St. Augustine puts it, "in us without us") which, while they do not necessitate our choices, do influence them more or less strongly. Nor can we avoid the conclusion that certain psychological types seem to be less fitted by nature to lead stable, balanced and responsible moral lives. Such people should be encouraged to hope in the understanding love and mercy of a God aware of the personal environmental and hereditary factors of their total history going all the way back to Adam. Those whom unfortunate childhoods have marked with overdeveloped aggressiveness and insufficient liberty in their emotional life must always cling to the hand of God even when the darkness presses exceedingly close. Such sinners must recognize themselves as sinners in the presence of the mystery of holiness and call upon the helping God.

In the very depths of his being, at the point which mystics refer to as his "heart," man must make a fundamental option for himself or for God. And it is the depths of the heart which Christ demands. It is possible that even he whose exterior life is scarcely conformed to the objective moral law may yet have good reason to hope in the helping God. The sinner is not normally in a position to judge his own life. The patience that God calls upon him to exercise in dealing with others must also be directed towards himself. God calls to a total transformation of one's life. But God is aware of all the conditions that hedge and limit the possibility of such transformation in the psychologically afflicted. Whatever be the past, however heavily it weighs upon the sinner, there is still a future of sanctity open to him if he will freely meet the liberty of God extending redemptive grace to him. A certain maturity is required in the order of spirit, just as in the biological order, for the possibility of either holiness or sin. Liberty and grace play their roles at the very depths of man's personal life in the pre-given situations in which he finds himself. The tangle of personal motivations is not easily unravelled, and the priest with his long confessional experience is usually aware of this fact. For grace to make its effects felt in the wounded psychologies of which we are speaking, it must express itself less in a visible success than in a constant, loving, trusting fidelity in effort. Every sinner is called upon to exert the full measure of his liberty towards fulfilling the whole objective law of God. When liberty is hindered by a neurosis which clouds the evaluative faculties, man must exert decisive effort in those sectors of the battle in which he has freedom. Fidelity to the commands of God and the appeals of the Spirit will in some cases be evident less in measurable success than in the continued effort to collaborate with grace. It is not advisable to approach the sinner with so legalistic a viewpoint that the infused virtue of hope is dried up within his soul. Rather, the theologian must make the sinner aware that even without grace, the cultivation of hope, the sense of dependence upon God, the humble longing to fufill God's will in seemingly impossible conditions, must still be pursued. In such cases, we can clearly hope, without presumption, that God will reward the good will of the sinner by straightening his path, closing the gap between what he sincerely longs to be and what he is.[11]

Chapter 6

GROWTH IN CHRIST

6

Growth in Christ

The law of self-denial is fundamental to Christian asceticism. As a Christian attitude the spirit of self-denial in no way implies a radical pessimism concerning the meaning of nature, of creaturely reality or of man himself. It is simply a realistic evaluation of the actual situation of man who has been wounded by original sin, at least in an extrinsic fashion, and has thereafter been redeemed by the grace of Christ and commissioned to co-operate with the crucified Savior in his own redemption. Because of sin the spiritual development of man can no longer be envisaged simply as a natural and linear growth or education. It must also be seen as a re-education, a re-unification, and a reconstruction. For in order to foster that valid or well-ordered self-love of which St. Thomas speaks, man must realistically face the fact that spiritual unity can be acquired only by putting to the sword that false self-love which is variously called selfishness, egotism, self-indulgence or self-seeking.

Man is a creature with a composite nature, and his laborious attempts to give himself wholly to God are constantly inhibited by a certain dualism rooted in the very structure of his being. It is hard for him to gather himself up in one splendid gesture, for his personal decisions do not easily penetrate the whole length and breadth of his being. Total self-possession is an ideal very difficult to realize, for we never succeed in making every stratum of ourselves the pure expression of what we truly wish to be. There is always a lag; we are always to a greater or lesser extent defied by the principle of concupiscence within us which proves resistant to the personal free decision to give oneself wholly to God. Even in the best of men there are always elements which do not correspond to the free decision but which remain unmanageable and obstinate. Try as he will to personalize and stamp with his freedom all of himself, even the saint finds resistances within the self which refuse to be caught up by his freedom, and so not even the saint possesses and masters himself perfectly in any one act. Consequently he too is unable to give himself over to the Infinite wholly in any one act but must repeat his donation to God innumerable times throughout his life.[1]

THE LAW OF LIFE

The resistances of our dualistic nature to this effort to give ourselves wholly to God explain in part our need of self-denial. It is self-denial that helps the spirit to close the gap between what one seeks by his freedom and what he achieves, partially and deficiently. Self-denial is needed as a corrective to that spontaneous, amoral tendency of our dualistic nature to impede the total disposition of self with regard to the Infinite God. Abnegation strengthens freedom to the point where we are gradually more able to be ourselves, to dispose of ourselves fully and wholly. Bit by bit it "personalizes" our nature. In the lives of the saints we often encounter striking examples of the docility of a man's whole being to the free choice of his will, a rare quality laboriously and painfully acquired through years of self-denial motivated by charity. The saints have come to the liberty of the children of God, and they have also come to a more fully natural freedom. But they have come to it over an austere road and through persistent efforts at unifying their nature by resistance to concupiscence—a resistance firmly spelled out in terms of an active opposition to the selfish, egotistic, pleasure-bent trend of their composite nature. From Paul to Augustine to the saints of the twentieth century, these heroic men and women remind us incessantly of that steely lesson of mortification and self-denial because their personal experiences have taught them that the freedom to love God completely is acquired slowly and at the cost of relentless resistance to egotism and false self-love.

The fundamental optimism of Christianity shines forth in the realization that self-denial does not limit or impair genuine human and spiritual values but rather nourishes them and helps them mature and flower. The law of developing life is quite simply a pattern of death to the forces that impede development of life. For when man seeks himself exclusively in his activities, even his human personality deteriorates, and surely grace cannot exercise its own inner laws of expansion unless it has room to do so. But it is precisely such room that self-denial wins. Our Lord insisted so often and so strongly upon this principle of self-denial that we can hardly ignore it with comfort. Early in his public life He warned us that unless a man denied himself he could not become one of His disciples. On another occasion He warned that unless the grain of wheat dies, itself remains alone. He declared of Himself that it was necessary that He should suffer and die. On the occasion of the Sermon on the Mount He hailed as blessed those who are poor in spirit, those who are hungry and thirsty for justice' sake, those who suffer and who weep. This is the corrective that He would apply to an unbalanced humanism which would rashly act as if the resurrection of the flesh had already happened. Christian humanism never forgets the cross. Christ makes the point clearly: one does not gain the pearl of great price without the loss of all one possesses; one does not savor the ointment of the alabaster box without breaking it open. The law of growth, of developing life, is renouncement, death.

In the history of salvation does not God point to this same lesson? Israel was content to remain Israel, and in thus refusing to surpass herself, she ceased to be the New Israel, she failed to become the new humanity. God's action throughout history teaches the identical lesson. Is not the principle of *kenosis,* the "pouring out" of self, at the source of the new life Jesus announced that He had come to bring? In the infant Church this same law of development through renunciation is often in evidence. The Church renounces all Judaizing tendencies and expands as the mustard seed; Paul renounces the ancient faith and becomes all things, even to the Israelites. The Kingdom of God is infinite, and entrance into it is made through renouncement of limits, of the finite. As Blondel has remarked, the most authentic method for possessing the Infinite is still the classic Christian method . . . dispossessing oneself of what is not the Infinite: the classical road of the cross. Or, as T. S. Eliot put it, consciously echoing John of the Cross: "In order to possess what you do not possess, you must go by way of dispossession." To be great one must cease to be small. One must cease to be immured in egotism and must expand one's interests to embrace the interests of the Church. Without this death to self-seeking there is no possibility of expanding in the order of grace. St. Augustine summed it up in a sentence: "Two forms of love have constructed two cities; the love of self to the contempt of God has built the earthly city and the love of God to the contempt of self has built the Heavenly City."[2]

This law of development through mystical death or self-denial presides at the very door of our spiritual life. Does not Baptism engraft us onto the new life of Christ by plunging us mystically into the death of Christ and dedicating us to the continued mystical death to self? For we are obliged to foster the new life of grace by renouncing sin and the forces of destruction. By dedicating us to a social life in the Church Baptism already attacks excessive selfishness, individualism and egotism. Baptism dedicates us to denial of the narrower vision of egotism and opens up perspectives of social charity, justice and concern with others. Penance, as a second Baptism, renews our renouncement and our consecration to the new life. It is the same law of life through death that is operative here.

Confirmation further increases this death to self since it consecrates us to a social, sacerdotal holiness where our concerns are enlarged to include active interest in the concerns of the whole Church. The Eucharist, too, conspicuously embodies this same law of life: renouncement of self. For the Eucharist unites us to Christ the Savior, who was Savior *as Victim.* The reception of the Eucharist thus serves to remind us that the passion of Christ is not finished forever but is renewed in His mystical prolongations, ourselves. Marriage and the sacrament of Orders also have this same transcendent function of liberating the individual from selfishness and dedicating him to the species, to the new humanity which Christ has come to create. In a word, all the sacraments imply social concerns and social interests, preoccupations and attitudes which demand the death of selfishness and self-seeking.

Our Lord has greatly insisted upon this law of self-denial and renouncement, and He has insisted upon it because it is a necessary precondition to the expansion of the divine life given in Baptism. It seems as though each of man's free acts is fought over by nature and by grace, and unless man is established in the conviction that he must mortify self, his nature—with its downward trend of concupiscence—usually wins the day. When a man seeks himself, all too often he ends by finding only himself, and self simply cannot satisfy even the natural man. The Christian must engage in an unremitting effort to substitute God and His concerns for self as the center of his life, or he is doomed to unhappiness. It is well to recall the sobering words of Lallemant: "We spend whole years, and often a whole life, in bargaining whether we shall give ourselves wholly to God . . . We must renounce, then, once and for all, all our own interests and all our own satisfactions, all our own designs and all our own choices, that we may henceforth be dependent only on the good pleasure of God, and resign ourselves entirely into His hands." Asceticism aims to paralyze egotism, pleasure-seeking and unenlightened self-love. Only when these motive forces have been replaced with the dynamism of grace can the soul experience the energy and enthusiasm in God's service which, under the impulse of His inspiration, it longs for.

The law of death to self is only mortifying in appearance. Still, it requires a certain amount of experience of the spiritual life before we can fully realize that the law of renunciation is really an affirmation of life. Before that experience is acquired the soul is expected to live in the domain of faith, accepting on the word of faith the truth that what God asks of us is that we walk the right path to human and divine happiness. As God never requires of the soul anything irrational, neither does He require anything that militates against the soul's happiness *as spirit*. This affirmation must be quietly accepted upon faith, when the evidence of the senses is not given. When Jesus announced the ignominious death He was to die upon the cross, the apostles were stupefied and almost scandalized. But Christian experience of the triumph of the cross and resurrection is now plainly evident to all, and the Christian today is heir to generations of social experience of the fittingness of the folly of the cross. Nevertheless we often repeat the fear and amazement of the apostles. Today we must affirm upon faith, even before our experience of it as a law of life, that self-denial opens the heart to the meaning of generosity and love, and to the significance of the Infinite in our lives.

THE LAW OF LOVE

Nietzsche accused Christianity of canonizing mediocrity. According to him Christianity produced a race of slaves and not a race of supermen. If this were true, Christianity would be a religion of negation and resignation, of passivity and infantilism, a simple prophylactic of salvation for the individual, a spiritual opium for the dispossessed of this world.[3]

So gross a misunderstanding of Christianity could never have come into being if this philosopher had ever considered the meaning of self-denial in Christian experience. Christianity is above all a *social* religion and ours is a communal hope for a communal salvation. Far from being an opium, Christianity requires the vision and the strength to measure values and to hierarchize them according to their objective dignity. It is a religion for the strong; the kingdom of heaven suffereth violence and the violent bear it away. The true disciples of Jesus have lived fully and have died fully. They have not been compromisers, and because they have not, they have fulfilled even their human destinies in the supreme fashion. It is not the timid and the mediocre souls who bear the name of Christian most naturally, but those who have fought with tenacity and courage the great battle on the lasting front of egotism and selfishness. These were aware that a man finds his life by losing it and that even in the natural order "spirit" or "person" has been defined as a capacity for self-donation and for self-transcendence. Nature reflects grace in this law of self-donation for self-fulfillment. Man becomes himself fully by donating himself fully to another. But such a donation is made up of a multitude of little fidelities day by day.

Henri Bergson has said that we are living in an aphrodisiac civilization. It is certainly evident to the most casual observer of our American scene that the search for pleasure has become dominant in our culture. Against such a trend the Christian is called upon to take a decisive stand and to witness the superiority of values higher than pleasure. "Always bearing about in our bodies the mortification of Jesus, that the life also of Jesus may be made manifest in our bodies." The glory of the Christian is "the cross of our Lord Jesus Christ, through which the world stands crucified to me, and I to the world."

The Christian life that is not marked by self-denial and mortification is a life at opposition with itself and doomed to dissatisfaction and unhappiness. It could not be otherwise. Mediocrity does not satisfy. A life marked by fear of sacrifice gradually assumes a disunified aspect. It becomes a dialectic of giving and refusing; contradictory choices alternate; life then becomes structured by an unhealthy discontinuity and inconsistency. A life parcelled out between the finite and the Infinite, between creatures and God, between flesh and spirit becomes a pale parody of the Christian life. The individual who wishes to be neither hot nor cold but comfortably tepid, installed in a quasi-automatic routine of religious life, is fated for disunity. To retreat before anticipated sacrifice is to ignore the heroic implications of the Christian life.

It should be quite clear that in the plan of Christian life self-denial and sacrifice must be present. Grace and the cross have an affinity for one another which cannot be denied. Our humanism is a humanism that is crucified. Jesus, the source of grace, is typically represented on the cross; from the cross springs the new nature that elevates and heals. We are "more marvellously re-made" to be sure, but "the Author and Finisher of our faith" was crucified. Holiness is progressive identification with Christ, and if it is to be redemptive we must remember that redemption involves the payment of a price.

It is in this perspective of our vocation to holiness and progress in life that we must regard the fundamental law of Christian asceticism: progress in life through death to selfishness, progress in charity through self-denial. It is from this point of view that we must honestly reflect upon our devotion to comfort, to pleasure, to self-satisfaction and self-indulgence.

It is, no doubt, a personal matter for each of us to appraise his own life. Yet as we do so, which of us would not find poignant the words of a great Catholic layman, François Mauriac, who once wrote: "We have spent our lives forming attachments, that is the truth of the matter—and there would be nothing extraordinary or scandalous about this if we did not at the same time spend our lives acknowledging a crucified God who asks His disciples to leave everything and take up His cross to follow Him."

THE LAW OF LIBERTY

Christ posed the problem of human liberty in a fashion which must have seemed novel to the ancient world. Before His coming men believed it their task to develop liberty by submitting the entire world to their own choices and exploiting it as fully as possible. In place of this Christ suggested a renouncement which is total, affecting the length and breadth of man's life. This demands a certain psychological "distance" from all the pre-existent circumstances in our human situation. A man enters the world not by his own choice but by the choice of God, and there he finds himself in a situation which precedes him. He does not create his own social, familial, racial, civil, national, biological or sex characteristics. These are given him by God, and it is out of these that he must gradually construct his spiritual liberty. Despite the fact that many circumstances are necessarily imposed upon him, liberty of choice is given to him as a means to re-create his situation within the limits of possibility. One central choice—for example, of a vocation or a profession—might orientate man's whole life in a new direction and unify all less important choices. What Christ suggests is that we free ourselves from attachment to these pre-given circumstances and re-create our liberty in imitation of the divine creation—from nothing, and by the word of God. For the metaphysical origin of all created reality is nothingness and God's creative word. And it is to this focal point that Christ directs us in mortification and abnegation.[4]

The mortified man thus assumes the risk of the divine

adventure, re-creating a new world from nothingness and the will of God. Every decision of a liberty constantly in process necessarily points towards the future and is an act of faith touched with hope, not simply a blind submission to fate. God freely created the world out of love. The mortified man re-creates some shadow of this love in his human liberty, for he shares in the creative love of God by reconstructing his own individual world and making Christ its center. The process of abnegation therefore coincides with a process of developing liberty. Its only constraint is the love of Christ, drawing man to reconstruct his own personality. The measure of liberty is proportionate to the amount of our self-denial. Even a pagan freed from slavery to a degrading passion registers the freedom that self-denial brings.

But the Christian's self-denial is not ordered to an iron mastery of self. This would deny his needy human condition and create a *mystique* of stoicism. Christian detachment demands much humility and meekness. It is no cult of selfishness or stony voluntarism, but it walks the road of humiliation without bitterness, trusting in Christ. Christian detachment moreover goes deeper into all the strata of man's life than could any pagan stoicism. We do not merely abandon exterior power, riches, influence; this would be but a negative and superficial way of acting. Instead we abandon all possessions in complete and open surrender of self to God. In the exercise of abnegation one gains one's own liberty, freeing it from the compromises of earthly attachment. Abnegation forms us to the liberty of the children of God, greater submission to the divine will.

Liberty thus becomes transformed, detached, and doubly active in this world.[5]

The grammatical construction of the phrase "If a man wishes to be my disciple, let him renounce himself" is extremely interesting. The verb "deny oneself"—in the Latin, *abneget*—seems never to have been employed as a reflex verb before Christ so used it.[6] This notion of the denial of one's self signalizes the introduction of a new idea by the use of this new term. The Latin noun *abnegatio* is exclusively Christian in its origin. It appears to have been first employed by St. Jerome to signify self-denial. We ought also to note that the word found in the Greek text is the same as that which Christ employed when he said that Peter would deny Him thrice. St. John Chrysostom said, "To deny oneself is to have nothing more in common with one's self; it is as though one were a stranger to oneself." It is precisely this essential liberty, the deepest part of man, his "heart," which Christ wishes to seize by renouncement. When Christian ascetical writers translate denial of self as a renunciation of one's will they imply this idea.

All these expressions point to a revelation concerning the very meaning of man. Philosophically, they might be astonishing if one did not recall that man reaches his full autonomy and liberty by transcending himself. The instinct of self-preservation by which man constantly seeks to preserve life and possessions must be renounced and a new principle put in its place. Man is now no longer himself. Rather his whole life will be projected upon Another and he will despoil himself in favor of Another, Christ. More exactly, he will no longer live from himself but will accept his life as a gift from Another. Self-denial thus has as its purpose to found a free community in which one simultaneously loses himself and gains himself, since he is supported by God.

The process of self-denial is difficult, but it ends in a freedom which puts aside all hopes and projects not suggested by Christ. Man then becomes disengaged from empty occupations, and eventually is seized in his very being by the supernatural action of Another. A transforming union of love takes place. This transformation, begun by a detachment which was sometimes rough and even brutal, ends at last in joy. It is interesting to note that the Fathers of the Church have so frequently aligned with Christ's text on mortification the cry of St. Paul, "I live, now not I, but Christ lives in me." They grasped the truth that Christian abnegation ends in a transforming union of one's very existence. In the natural order the Pauline statement would only be a bold metaphor, but in the case of Christian abnegation, there is a genuine quasi-identification of a completely new order—that of the supernatural—between Christ and the mortified soul. The person once immured within himself is genuinely touched through mortification, freed and opened to Christ. This is a reflection, an image of the trinitarian mutual inhabitation, Christ and the soul inhabiting one another in a fashion which defies all spatial representation.[7]

Our precise aim in depriving ourselves of material and spiritual possessions is to love Christ more. Since it is by getting rid of what one has that one changes what one is, thanks to mortification a new man is gradually made and the old man who foolishly identified himself with inferior objects is put off. To help us understand that one can renounce what one is only by renouncing what one has, Christ spoke of renunciation of glory, of the first place, of the banquet, of riches, of one's family, and of sleep. The measure proposed by Christ is the measure of constant growth. Thus there is no end to the task of renunciation until the moment of death. Death is the ultimate renunciation, for here one consecrates the entire gift of his being to God. Renouncing all the past and the entire world one cleaves to God. In the supreme cry upon the cross the moment before His death, Christ effected a consummation of all His past renouncements as they had unrolled in the succession of time. So it is with us. We renounce ourselves daily, and the final renunciation is of this world and human life itself.

The whole material universe itself shares in this renunciation, for the realization of the full Christ is conditioned upon the totality of renunciations in all His members. The universe itself must be denied if it is to be fulfilled. Otherwise it will fall back on itself in a materialistic fashion.[8] To realize its genuine destiny, the universe itself must go through a final catastrophe which is not arbitrary, but which is required by the nature of things. This transformation requires denial and destruction as a prelude. The law is always the same: renunciation operates a progressive interior death. Yet Christian abnegation is penetrated with hope and orientated towards a glorious future, especially towards those most glorious events: the resurrection of the body, the restoration of the world, and the Parousia.

SUMMARY

All through life, then, we continue the task of mortification. Our past renunciations cannot subsist except at the price of present renunciations. No matter how great the sacrifices of the past, unless we sacrifice ourselves today, the will turns in on itself. Hence each new day brings its problem of adaptation to maintain the prior decision. Abnegation is a general disposition presiding over all our acts in time. The radiant face of Christian abnegation already points towards eternity.

As it was with the death of Christ, which depended upon a conjunction of historical circumstances and human depravity, so it will be with the trials of life, which will often be due to circumstances outside our control so that we can only affirm our liberty by accepting these conditions. We need the mediation of temporal circumstances and of people outside ourselves to mortify ourselves. There is no other condition possible for the exercise of human liberty in search of mortification. It must express itself in a context of exterior determinism which acts as a field for personal choices. Just as Christ wished to sacrifice Himself in the midst of time and among men, so too His disciple must daily come to grips with his own history dependent upon those about him. The circumstance of the precise milieu itself determines the cross which each man must carry. In this sense, renunciation is fully incarnational.

The constancy of mortification is related to the very nature of love itself. Love demands a constant renouncement if it is to grow. A love which attempts to remain at its present stage of development is unfaithful to itself. Supernatural love, like natural, is a constant rhythm of progress and self-denial. Renunciation is part of its daily rhythm. Christ, who wishes a fruitful love worthy of our liberty, expects of us fidelity in renunciation. Each day offers us the opportunity of a refusal or a further gift. What counts is the long fidelity, the daily sacrifice lest love should die of inactivity. Mortification exercises so unifying an action upon our lives that life itself becomes the preface to an eternity. For the one love here played out in a multiplicity of acts has gradually unified our life even unto the joy of the heavenly vision forever.

Chapter 7

THE WORK OF THE CHRISTIAN

7

The Work of the Christian

Since so much of our existence is occupied with work it is perhaps well to examine the meaning of work in a Christian universe. Is work simply imposed by God that we may suffer and thus do penance for our sins? Is work in our Christian world in any sense a co-operation with God? Is work charged with hope? Is work simply a way of gaining one's livelihood, or does it have some divine significance? Finally, are they correct who speak of work as a task to be endured before we can begin the serious business of life—enjoyment, the fulfillment of personal talents, contemplation and prayer?

WORK IN THE OLD TESTAMENT

To grasp something of the Christian significance of work it is helpful to see it first in its biblical perspective. The first thing that astonishes the biblical historian when he studies the nature of work is the important fact that God Himself is represented in the Bible as a worker. From the very first pages we see that God acts to realize a work. Genesis reveals to us God's work of creation as effortless activity, in startling contrast to the cosmogonies of the surrounding Semitic civilizations. Yahweh undertakes to create the universe and finds outside Himself no resistance to His will. With a supernal transcendence He summons into existence this glorious universe, and it obeys Him. It is His work, and He rests on the seventh day from His labor.

This earth is the product of God's omnipotence, and He is pleased to compare Himself with the toiling artisan. The sea is His, for He has made it, and with His hands He has formed the dry land. The creation cycle ends with the striking picture of the omnipotent laborer almost at the service of His creatures. He is the supreme toiler, the divine "potter," the builder of the universe molding this world, shaping humanity and its framework, the earth, to His will. Here is the beginning of a theology of labor.

Elsewhere in the Bible it is clear that God labors to mold His chosen people. But God finds Himself open to resistance from the human liberty He has created. For man can utter his Yes or No to God. Yet in some mysterious fashion God remains the sovereign master over this human world too. He uses kings to accomplish His purposes, He makes and breaks empires at His will. He is independent of all human instruments in completing the construction of the family of His choice. We note, however, that once the question of the formation of a family is raised the divine work takes on a new aspect. The effortless joy that marked the creation of the physical universe is no longer manifest in Scripture when God begins this task of forming a people to His desires. Here a new element seems to enter, the element of fatigue, suffering, effort, trouble.

Isaias gives us many bold images to show God engaged, as it were, in effortful work. He compares Yahweh to a harvester treading his grapes, to a soldier who leads an exhausting life, to a farmer cultivating a fruitless vine. This is, of course, the history of the people of Israel, the people of God's choice, who have chosen to make His work a seemingly barren struggle. Isaias has an even stronger image in which he speaks of God laboring like a woman in childbirth, groaning with the sorrows of childbirth in the formation of His people. God puts energy into His task and experiences something like suffering and fatigue. When we look ahead to the New Testament and think of Christ the great toiler, bending to His redemptive task, stained with His own blood, we understand the images of the Old Testament where Yahweh appears worn out with the battle for His rebel people, returning at evening, a solitary harvester, his garments dyed red with the grapes He has trod alone. Work, in the biblical perspective, is not always effortless. It is redemptive, and when the redemptive note enters, there enters the idea of pain, suffering, effort.[1]

The opening chapters of Genesis also show us Adam set to the task of cultivating the paradise which God has given him. All the beasts of the fields come before Adam and he calls them by name; he knows their essence and takes charge of the garden which God has entrusted to him. After the fall, the earth will bring forth thorns and thistles, but even before the fall, man is obliged to work at his garden. Before the fall, however, work is simply a joyous expression of man's personality, a spontaneous activity free from all punitive character. After the fall it takes on the character of a punishment. Centuries later, after the redemption, it will also assume the nature of a liberation, a redemptive activity.

The attitude of the Bible with regard to work is quite different from what we find in pagan civilizations. To the pagan, work was a universal burden for the lower classes and the slaves. Class distinctions, of course, were very marked. At the summit of society were the kings and rulers, who under no circumstance debased themselves by manual work. At the base of pre-Christian society were the slaves and artisans, who undertook tremendous "public works" under the most inhuman conditions. Generally speaking, the purpose of these enormous works of pagan civilization was pride, vainglory. Occasionally they served the common good, but the workers who undertook these tasks must have felt strongly the punitive character of work. Fatigue, suffering, effort—this was the lot of the worker, while the superior class enjoyed peace, leisure, *dolce far niente.* The spiritual climate in which were constructed the pyramids of Egypt and the hanging gardens of Babylon was not such as to suggest that work itself was an expression of the worker's personality. Instead, it was an imposed suffering undergone for the profit of the fortunate few.

Greece and Rome were not much different in this respect from the other pagan civilizations. In fact, the most intelligent writers of Greece and Rome considered slavery a normal circumstance of life. Zenophon, for example, advises us to treat slaves with kindness and to alternate blows with food in order to assure better work. Aristotle takes it for granted that the slave lacks free will, is really not quite human. Work was a burden which prevented man from freeing his personality for contemplation, philosophy or the tasks of politics. Greco-Roman society was organized completely around the notion of slavery, and although the slaves were frequently treated with kindness, it seems that no one questioned slavery as an institution. One has only to glance at the deities which inhabit the temples of Greece and Rome to see that this approach to work was confirmed by religion. The divine ideal, and consequently the human ideal, is that of leisure and ease.[2]

This is in sharp contrast to the idea of work revealed in the Old Testament. Since God Himself had worked, the Hebrew could not possibly conceive of work as something reserved to slaves and those unfit for higher tasks. Without a doubt there was much social inequality among the Jews, but the prophets were there to recall to men the common destiny of material goods and to forbid treating the worker or the slave unjustly. The Mosaic law admitted slavery, but slavery, as it was practiced among the Jews, did not manifest the same degrading character that it had among pagan peoples.

Labor itself was respected in the Bible. Job, for instance, tells us that man is born to labor as the bird is born to fly. Many of the prophets of the Old Testament were chosen by God from among the laboring classes, the shepherds. Evidently they were among the healthiest of the Jewish people. All through Jewish history one hears the piping of shepherds and the calling of sheep, and there is no time at which manual labor was ever despised by the Hebrew. Even the rabbis occasionally had a manual trade in addition to their learned pursuits. Palestine in particular honored the agricultural worker, and it was customary to greet the laborers in the fields with blessings. Honest toil was honored by God Himself, since He chose such workers as Saul and David for a royal destiny. The Bible itself approves of diligence and disapproves of idleness. The lazy man is warned to observe the ways of the ant and learn wisdom from him; there is praise for the model housewife who has looked well to the needs of her house and who has not eaten her bread in idleness. The Book of Proverbs urges men to work and dwells upon the natural returns of honest industry; the hand of the laborious man begets riches and he shall know abundance.

This is in striking contrast to the ancient dynasties such as Babylon. Scholars have calculated that thirty million bricks were used in the construction of certain temples of Babylonian antiquity. Most of this labor was accomplished by purely human force. Horses were deemed too noble for the task of drawing wood and stone but captives and slaves were not. The hanging gardens of Babylon must have been constructed in sweat and blood; the pyramids of Egypt, some of which still exist, give us an idea of the stupendous labor involved in building them. Herodotus suggests, concerning one of them, that the workers labored for thirty years in relays of one hundred thousand.[3] Ten years were devoted to the construction of the road along which the blocks of stone were to be drawn. Without the aid of animals or machines six million tons of stone were set in place by human hands to build this monstrous memorial to human vanity.

In Palestine, too, the viewpoint of the law with regard to the slave was quite different from that of pagan countries. From the beginning the slave was to be introduced into the household of God so that even he might have applied to him the rite of the covenant and become aware that before God there is no distinction of slave and free. No slave could be looked upon as a possession existing purely for his master's advantage. The slave too had rights before God, and Israel was constantly reminded of this by the prophets. To the slave was also allowed the joy of the Sabbath rest, an institution unknown in the pagan world. Divine Law provided that the Hebrew slave could not be put to degrading tasks and that he had to be treated with kindness and courtesy. It is important also to note that a slave could not be kept in bondage beyond six years. However, if he chose freely to remain with his master he was not to be driven out, but had the right to enjoy protection in the household he had served. In the seventh year, if he chose to go free, he was to be liberated, and when free he was not to go empty-handed but was to receive from the master gifts of wine, food and cattle.

The Book of Leviticus introduces a law in favor of the Hebrew slave, which is known as the year of Jubilee. By it every fiftieth year all Hebrew slaves were to be unconditionally freed and allowed to depart with their wives and children. Moreover, a Hebrew servant was freed when his master died without male heir in the direct line. Hebrews frequently entered voluntarily into slavery to escape poverty and ensure themselves regular employment. Evidently slavery did not imply the degradation or penury which it had among other primitive peoples. Again, the Hebrews could not be forced into slavery, except as a punishment for crime. Women slaves too, according to the law of Palestine, were carefully provided for and could not be treated according to the whims of the master.

The Hebrew master was hedged about in many ways by divine commandments to prevent arbitrary treatment of slaves. This attitude is in sharp contrast to that of paganism in which slaves were classed with beasts of burden or "instruments endowed with life," as Aristotle called them. It was forbidden to sell Hebrew slaves to pagan nations lest they be tempted to apostasy. If one Hebrew sold another to a Gentile, he was forced not only to redeem him at whatever price the new master asked, but was also obliged to set him free immediately. Even captives were to be treated justly, and this treatment was regulated by law. Women captives might be married, but the law laid down specific conditions for their protection. Frequently slaves fled to Israel in order to make themselves slaves to Jewish masters, so protected was the Hebrew slave, and it is almost unheard of in Jewish history to read of slaves fleeing Hebrew masters.[4]

A certain esteem for manual work is thus evident in the Jewish traditions, and we read in the Bible of a long procession of workers who gained their livelihood through hard and honest labor.

Then, too, the terror of invasion by the Gentiles, the sadness of exile, the freedom bought at the price of slavery in Egypt taught the Jew a certain moderation with regard to great human enterprises. He learned to regard work as a vital necessity, sometimes enjoyable and sometimes laborious, but always a law of nature. Laziness was reprobated, for it was the mother of sin. A man was expected to keep his household alive but his ambitions moderate, for riches tended to render one unjust, sefish, hard and avaricious. He was obliged to labor for the sake of his family and children, but the mad desire for work which possesses modern civilization was not approved of in Israel. Egypt had taught the sad lesson that grandiose projects were generally at the expense of the little people of the world.

WORK IN THE NEW TESTAMENT

When we come to the New Testament we find that detachment from this world's goods is stressed but that work is also praised. Jesus Himself was a worker. He grew in age, in knowledge and wisdom, and He learned His trade from Joseph. While work is not accented in the New Testament as strongly as is detachment from the goods of this world, there is always the supernal figure of Christ who labors for the small community of Nazareth. It is work that brought Him fatigue, but also the joy of producing something for the human community in which He lived. The work of Christ was not simply an expiation, it was a work of genuine fraternal charity. Later He would work in the apostolate; always and above all He works at our redemption.

We meet in the figure of Christ the same contrast between joyous and suffering work that we met in the work of God. When Christ encounters the rebellious will of mankind, His work becomes laborious, wearying. He wrestles with an unwilling humanity, the redemption is accompanied by effort and suffering, and the note of struggle prevails throughout the later months of Jesus' apostolic activity. Finally, He dies upon the cross, the great toiler who fulfilled the task for which He was sent into the world.

THE CHURCH AND WORK

The Church makes evident in her concern for work her fundamental respect for the material universe and for human values. While a certain withdrawal from the world is characteristic of Christianity and a certain penitential asceticism is dominant in Christian thought, still the Church has always approved human values. She has defended such values as the capacity of the intellect to come to knowledge, the freedom of the will, the legitimacy of marriage, and the value of the human body itself. Far from condemning the material world, she has spoken out in defense of matter and its dignity when it was under contemptuous attack by certain oriental philosophies. Speaking out of a revealed knowledge of the destiny of matter, she manifests Christ's presence in the universe.

A fundamental theme in much of the Old Testament is that the material universe is a visible manifestation of the invisible God. In the New Testament St. Paul tells us that the pagan can come to a knowledge of God from admiring the work of His creation. Further, the mystery of the Incarnation means that matter has been taken up into personal union with the Divinity. The eternal purpose of the Incarnation reorders all things towards Christ, having already effected a partial transformation of matter, which now groans for its complete redemption. Matter is no longer a brutal impersonal force. All the laws of this universe are unified in Christ, their center. St. Paul tells us that all things are recapitulated in Christ, and that "the new skies, and the new earth" bear a reference to the Incarnate Word. The simple material things of our human existence have ceased to be merely gross matter, and have become instead instruments of the salvific plan. Matter has been made the vessel of divine mercy in the Incarnation.

As a result, the material universe upon which we exert our labor has become, in a certain sense, our brother. Francis of Assisi strongly underscores this fraternal feeling towards earthly and material beings. Nevertheless, the earth requires a further transformation by us, in whom the Incarnation is prolonged. Not only does the world call forth our praise of God, leading us to a knowledge of His power and perfection, but it also invites us to transform it by our work. Consequently, work has now a creative and a re-creative aspect. It is no longer simply a mechanical force which we use to gain our living, for human liberty has been invited to enter into our work. In this sense work has a human value. Christian thought accepted joyously the perspective of work for man, because Genesis had indicated that this is a human duty. Moreover, Christ, the apostles, St. Paul, all had given us examples of work. It is in fact a command based on the authority of God and the power of the Church. No longer merely a necessity or an instinct, work has now the dignity of a moral value, since it is commanded by God.[5]

Some Christians, indeed, seem to think that work serves for nothing more than the painful fulfillment of this command of God. They remind us that civilizations are destined to wither away and therefore have no lasting importance for the Christian. God, however, does not impose tasks which have no inner significance. If He has imposed upon us this task of working, it must have some interior aspect of value for the Christian. It is true at least that the Christian by his work co-operates with God, the Creator of the material universe and of all visible things. The earth is, as it were, a vast and empty field awaiting the energy and initiative of man to transform it into a hospitable home. The earth has been given over to man that he may act as its guardian and bring it to a more complete material perfection. Human effort continued through the centuries thus furthers the divine intention with regard to the world. The discoveries of technology and science can all be used for the glory of God because, in the words of Pius XII, "they continue the work begun by the Creator." The Christian has become a sub-creator under the influence of God in his effort to render civilization more adaptable to mankind.

Work, moreover, has an important effect upon the human personality. It is through his activity that man becomes fully himself. Through action upon the world, through his work, he impregnates the material universe with his own intelligence and freedom, and in doing so, grows in the consciousness of his personal gifts and choices. For he becomes aware of his liberty inasmuch as he constructs his small universe according to his own will. Leo XIII has recalled to mankind the fact that work is frequently the measure of man's personal development. Made in the image of a creative God, man is naturally creative and enjoys expressing himself exteriorly.[6]

This is not to imply that all forms of work foster creative expression equally. In the human scheme of things work is often necessary, sometimes pleasurable, frequently painful, but it is also an attempt on the part of mankind to humanize the world and to construct a better social milieu. Doubtless this opens the way to pride, avarice, and the exploitation of others. But at the same time it offers man the possibility of controlling his natural laziness, of opening his soul to humility in his daily tasks, and of working for the human community in fraternal charity. It is true that work, by its painful quality, is an expiation for sin, but this is not its ultimate explanation. Neither is work a punishment arbitrarily inflicted upon man by an offended God. Suffering certainly enters into our human work as a consequence of sin, but that suffering is a salvific and redemptive suffering imposed by love to assist mankind in conquering the reign of sin. The man who works at his daily tasks for the love of God puts himself at the service of his neighbor, and also at the service of this world as it moves towards its destiny, a transformed universe, the new earth and new heavens of Isaias.

Man should grow, too, in his awareness of that Christian ideal of action which incorporates contemplation. We do not accept as normative the Greek idea that exclusively intellectual contemplation is the perfect human activity. Instead, perfection for most of us demands not only that contemplation overflow into activity but also that work be thoroughly penetrated by contemplation. Apostolic work is a principle of life, whose unity and meaningfulness arise out of the contemplation which it involves and fosters. We no longer believe that perfection requires that we withdraw from the work of the world, but we do believe that work and activity should be inspired by charity and executed in love. Not that activity can substitute in any way for that formal prayer which is demanded of all Christians, but that action upon this world, undertaken for the sake of God, should be formed by charity, directed to Christ and fulfilled in Him.[7]

Consequently, there exists today an asceticism of action. The period of formal prayer daily supplies the Christian with the spiritual energy needed that the life of action may be touched with the presence of the living God, elevated to the continual source of love. There is no reason to believe that God cannot be found, loved, and adored in action itself. In the meeting of men, in our social life, in our structuring of the visible universe we can live out a complete surrender to the God who made this universe. By actively seizing upon the external world we alter it, imposing upon it by our free choice a Christian destination and a Christian meaning. Our interior attitudes are thus incarnated in the external world. Among pagans work had been conceived as a sort of alienation from oneself, a necessary evil which contributed nothing to the fulfillment of the individual.[8] In the Christian world, however, work is a translation into external activity of the imitation of God's creative and redemptive acts. Based upon the very nature of man, work is neither self-estrangement nor abandonment of the interior life, but a normal human expression of interior spiritual attitudes. Because of man's incarnate nature, the perfection of his inner attitude finds its culmination in the tangible universe which surrounds him. This is normal because of the composite nature of man, which seeks to body forth its interior act. Often indeed it is through externalization that the inner act assumes its highest intensity. The saying of "I love you" frequently brings to its own intensity that interior love which preceded and caused it. So there is a vital interaction between the interior and the exterior acts of man which leads us to believe that work and activity have a positive function to perform in the development of his spiritual life.[9]

CONTEMPLATION AND ACTION

It is true a certain tension has always existed in the Christian life between prayer and activity. From the beginning, Christianity felt the call to asceticism, to the desert, to silence, interior prayer and the cultivation of the spiritual life through the exclusion of external works. Yet even in the early days of Christianity the monks of the desert were enjoined to make use of some external work. Activity, therefore, is highly desirable, for it serves to fulfill manhood, to express personality, to gain a living, and to help in the practice of fraternal charity. For if God has called upon us to love Him above all things, He has also enjoined us to love all Christians, the whole Mystical Body. The tension, then, between prayer and activity can be resolved by a theology of action. God demands of us that we fulfill our life in work, but He will be faithful in His assistance so that activity, far from hindering our interior life, will on the contrary foster and develop it. For if work is penetrated by a spirit of communication with God and fidelity to His suggestions, it will enable us to remain in contact with Him, who is present, as St. Ignatius says, in all things, working in them. We advance on the road towards union with Christ not merely by drawing back from the world but by advancing in fidelity to His commandments, and one of His commandments is to continue the redemption of the universe. Continual prayer is possible in the midst of action itself for the man who cultivates familiarity with God. Such a one will find God in all that he sees and does. This is Christian realism, for God actually is present in all things, and a cultivation of His presence is a form of prayer in which man meets God in an activity penetrated by the spirit of love and service towards the Mystical Body.

It is evident that one must carefully develop his capacity to find God in all of life's situations. For prayer and work have a reciprocal influence. As we work we find new material for prayer; we pray to be able to continue work with those inner dispositions of humility, submission, generosity and patience for which it calls. Further, prayer is the condition of fruitful work, quickening within us the sources of strength to approach our work with love.

Obviously, also, the soul at work must try to keep itself attentive to the purpose of its labor. We extend the kingdom of God and the presence of God in this world by our activity. All our human tasks should be accomplished with a consciousness of the presence of God, who provides

Himself and the Mystical Body is reflected in the love we bear to the universe itself. By immersing ourselves in the great stream of love which flows from the heart of humanity towards the Eternal Father, we unite our intentions with the intentions of Christ as He worked in the vineyard. The Eternal Father constantly labors at the building of the Mystical Body, and we too take a serene share in that task which St. Denis has called the noblest of all works, collaborating with God for the redemption of souls.[10]

To believe that purely spiritual activity is the ideal of human sanctity is impossible since the Incarnation. All that man is should enter into his donation to God. This is completely congruent with the enfleshed nature of man's spirit. We should not attempt to withdraw from our incarnate condition as though God had made an error when He chose to enflesh our spirit. There is, of course, the danger that work will appeal to egotism or to love of riches, or that it will deteriorate into an exteriorized activity. However, faith in the presence of God, simple familiarity with God present in His universe, will help to unite activity and prayer. We must never forget the dual nature of man; he is body as well as soul; he has a divine vocation as well as a human nature to fulfill; he requires both activity and prayer. Although the tension between the two themes of withdrawal from the world and redemption of the world will never be completely transcended in this life, man must labor to unify himself, recalling that what is interior and moral has primacy over what is exterior and material. His interior activity tends to fulfill itself in external action which in turn reacts upon the interior. That type of moral conduct has the highest value before God in which not only the intention but the external execution also is excellent. Man is essentially human in his spirituality and consequently seeks expression in the exterior universe for his spiritual sentiments and choices. One should not, therefore, contrast pure interiority with pure exteriority; neither is actually possible for man. Nor is either the ideal. What one must attempt is the progressive resolution of the tension between interiority and exterior activity. This requires that we see our human activity in relationship to the God of Love who has created the world, who works within the world and who points it towards its redemption.

THE CHRISTIAN VINEYARD

We must labor to make of this world a happier homeland for humanity. For successful commitment to action and work, Christian asceticism insists upon the need of certain periods of the day for contemplation in response to the call of the divine will. But perfection consists in charity towards God and also towards the neighbor. In the present order we are more sure of our love for God when we devote prayer and activity to making this world a hospitable home for our neighbor. We may not so cultivate our individual lives as to forget the social implications of sanctity. The individual is not sanctified simply as an individual, although he may be damned as an individual. Work undertaken for the pure love of God purifies the whole man and unites interior and exterior. Work undertaken for the sanctification of others is a fulfillment of the highest vocation of man, a response to the most intimate desires of the

Christian heart. It is permissible to leave prayer temporarily for charity; it is even obligatory upon occasions to do so. Action for the sake of glorifying God is a highly desirable way of praising God. As God's glory consists primarily in the communication to creatures of His goodness and the manifestation by creatures of His goodness, so the relationship of the creature to his Creator should be an attitude of loving recognition of the presence of God in all creaturedom. This is a high form of praise by which the universe is rendered eloquent, capable of joining with us in the praise of God.

One must, of course, never subvert the divine order of things, attempting to serve the neighbor at the expense of the commands of God or of what God demands in the way of adoration directed immediately towards Him. But if we act with an authentic intention, submitting ourselves to God in activity and cultivating His presence, we are established in the realism of Christianity. Our life and work can become so saturated with the presence of God that it is never lost, even in the most intense activity. This is, of course, an ideal towards which the ordinary man must strive, the term towards which he must at least direct himself. Although we cannot always think explicitly of God during work, a sense of His loving presence is the formative background against which our activity should be carried on. The human lover does not constantly think of his beloved, but the presence of the beloved is a super-actual background against which are played out his decisions and his actions. To animate to the depths our love of God we must from time to time retire from activity to grasp ourselves anew, summing ourselves up wholly, donating ourselves to God. Having done this, we may content ourselves in the security of faith that God is present in created reality. The activity which we carry on in this world is thus an imitation of the creative act which sent into this world the created universe and formed the body of the Redeemer of that universe.

The Christian is necessarily much preoccupied with this world. When, before His ascension, Christ declared "I will be with you all days, even till the consummation of the world," He did not mean until the destruction of the world but until its perfection, its fulfillment, its realization. The work of the Christian is therefore the salvation of the entire universe, be it the universe of idea, of value, of objects or of men. His function is to prolong the redemptive activity of the first Redeemer, Christ.

The Christian is intensely attached to this world because Christ is intensely attached to this world. By His Incarnation Christ bound Himself to this world, and He bound Himself irrevocably. From that moment on He is inscribed in our history, involved in our drama, one with us in our struggles and our victory.

The Christian's task, then, is to co-operate with Christ in extending the redemption to the entire cosmos. Each generation has the task of re-incarnating Christ in the particular secular culture of the day. The new discoveries of science, the new values of art and technocracy have need of men as interpreters if they are to fulfill their role in a sacramental universe. The Christian cannot remain on the sidelines of scientific research, of scholarship, of knowledge or of any form of human civilization or culture. If he does, he is on the sidelines of Christianity itself.

One of the most beautiful conquests of present day intelligence is the appreciation of the concept of process and history. We have arrived at the stage in human development when we are ready to conceive of a developing world, where we once imagined a frozen universe. History has invaded every discipline. Far from rejecting the presence of the Redeemer in this conception of the world, we find that His action on the world is even more intimate and constant than we had imagined. We envision now the evolution of a new world under the continued creative force of God.

In the preparation of this new world the Christian has his role as member of the Church. For the Church *is* Christ, extended in time and space, progressively assimilating to Himself the whole human community and progressively invading all of history and all of culture. Christ in His Church is directing the evolutionary process of this universe; He is the soul of its movement. He is engaged, in time, in sculpturing upon the universe the temporal face of the timeless God. His work and ours extend beyond the universe of men to the universe of the material cosmos, which itself hears echoes of His redemption as it once heard echoes of our fall. Christ has introduced, by His resurrection, a germ of renewal in this old earth, and through our efforts this renewal will spread to every domain of the physical universe.

We work and we study to dominate all human forms of activity and knowledge, that we may re-orientate all forms of human activity to Christ, their unique natural center, their sole explanatory unity. Man and this universe are intimately bound up together; not only man, but even this material cosmos, is destined to reveal again the face of God, and this is our human task in exploring the riches of human culture. The life of the Church is on the march in each generation, and it is the task of each generation to enlarge its horizons, to receive the acquisitions of the past, to welcome the advances of knowledge in the present, and to lead the way to the cultural frontiers of the future. For Christ extends His salvation to every creature, and all that is ancient wisdom and all that is new must be re-centered upon Christ, who is Wisdom ever ancient and ever new. In this perspective work is not a casual pastime, it is not primarily an economic necessity, it is not the self-contained self-development of a selfish epicurean. It is a share in the great Christian task, a collaboration with the redemptive labor of Christ. It is a glorification of the unique Prince of this world, Christ Incarnate, the same yesterday, today and forever. It is a share in the common Christian agony, the common Christian travail of a Church in labor till the redemption of every aspect of this world is achieved. When the task is fulfilled on the last day of triumph, every iota of what is being, every iota of what has being and is opposed to nothing, will reveal, will render up, the adorable face of Him who is—the Christ, in whom all things stand, by whom all things are made, to whom all things are ordered as to their heart and center.

NOTES

NOTES

INTRODUCTION: OLD AND NEW ORIENTATIONS

1. Cf. E. Masure, "Les tendances de la spiritualité contemporaine" in *La Spiritualité Catholique,* Paris, Le Rameau, 1953, ch. ix. The broad lines of contemporary spirituality are penetratingly analyzed each year in E. O'Brien's annual review of ascetical theology in *Theological Studies.*
2. C. V. Héris, *Spiritualité d'Amour,* Paris, Siloë, 1950; cf. also G. Gilleman, *Le Primat de la Charité en Théologie Morale,* Louvain, Nauwelaerts, 1952 and C. Spicq, *Agapé,* Louvain, Nauwelaerts, 1955.
3. The works of Mersch, Anger, Mura and Jürgensmeier are indications of this trend.
4. Cf. P. Pourrat, *Christian Spirituality,* Westminster, Newman, 1955, vol. iii, p. 319.
5. Cf. the author's *The World to Come,* New York, Sheed and Ward, 1958, pp. 157–168.
6. F. Cuttaz, *Our Life of Grace,* Chicago, Fides, 1958, introduction.
7. A. M. Roguet, *Christ Acts Through Sacraments,* Collegeville, Liturgical Press, 1958, pp. 84–87.
8. Yves de Montcheuil, *For Men of Action,* Chicago, Fides (n.d.), ch. vi.

9. Cf. the author's "Situational Morality," *Thought*, 1957–58 (32), pp. 343–347.

CHAPTER I: CHRIST THE CENTER

1. We wish to express our gratitude to the *Review for Religious* for allowing us to reprint certain material in this chapter which first appeared in the pages of that review.
2. P. Monier has admirably outlined this contrast in his *Exercises Spirituelles*, Paris, Vitte, 1952, pp. 503–507.
3. P. Henry, *Compléments de Christologie*, cours polycopié, Paris, Institut Catholique, 1952, ch. i.
4. P. Rousselot, *The Life of the Church*, London, Sheed and Ward, 1932, p. 27.
5. P. Blanchard, *Sainteté Aujourd'hui*, Paris, Desclée de Brouwer, 1954, pp. 95–97.
6. *Ibid.*, p. 98.

CHAPTER II: THE CHARITY OF CHRIST

1. We wish to express our gratitude to the Editor of *Sponsa Regis* for allowing us to reprint here some material which first appeared in that review.
2. T. Barrosse, "Christianity: Mystery of Love," *Catholic Biblical Quarterly*, vol. 20, pp. 138–139.
3. M. Ledoux, "A Philosophy of Relation to Others" in *Love of Our Neighbor*, Templegate, Ill., 1958, p. 104; p. 107.
4. E. Mersch, "Le plus grand des commandements," *N.R.T.*, 1947 (69), pp. 1022–1023.
5. *Ibid.*, p. 1024.
6. M. J. Le Guillou, "Brotherly Love and the Unifying of the Christian Life" in *Love of Our Neighbor*, p. 86.
7. A. Plé, "The Virtue of Charity" in *Love of Our Neighbor*, pp. 76–78.
8. *Ibid.*, pp. 140–142.
9. *Ibid.*, p. 141.

CHAPTER III: THE SUFFERING OF CHRIST

1. J. Gonsette, "Le Chrétien et la Souffrance," *N.R.T.*, 1954 (76), p. 485.
2. *Ibid.*, p. 489.
3. Y. de Montcheuil, *Leçons sur le Christ,* Paris, Ed. de L'Épi, 1949, ch. 10.
4. L. Charlier, "La Croix et la résurrection du Christ" in *La Souffrance, Valeur Chrétienne,* Paris, Castermann, 1957, pp. 198–201.
5. *Ibid.*, pp. 188–189.
6. *Ibid.*, p. 187.

CHAPTER IV: THE HUMILITY OF CHRIST

1. We wish to express our gratitude to the Editor of *Sponsa Regis* for permitting re-publication of certain material first published in that review.
2. R. Guardini, *The Lord,* Chicago, Regnery, 1954, p. 323.
3. P. Franssen, "Towards a Psychology of Divine Grace," *Lumen Vitae,* 1957 (XII), pp. 214–215.
4. R. Troisfontaines, "La Mort, épreuve de l'amour, condition de la fidélité" in *La Mort,* Paris, Lethielleux, 1948, pp. 40–46.
5. D. von Hildebrand, *True Morality and its Counterfeits,* New York, McKay, 1956, chs. i and ii.
6. *Ibid., loc. cit.*

CHAPTER V: HOPE AND FEAR

1. B. Olivier, "The Meaning of Christian Hope," *Lumen Vitae,* 1953 (9), p. 375.
2. *Ibid.*, pp. 378–379.
3. A. M. Carré, *Hope or Despair,* New York, Kenedy, 1957, pp. 29–33.
4. *Ibid.*, p. 24. Cf. also R. Bernard, *L'Espérance,* Paris, Ed. Mappus, 1957, ch. ii.
5. G. Marcel, *Homo Viator,* Chicago, Regnery, 1951, p. 60; pp. 61–63.

6. J. Rimaud, "Les psychologues contre la morale," *Etudes*, 1949 (263), pp. 3, 10–12.
7. P. Taymans d'Eypernon, *Le Mystère Primordial*, Paris, Desclée de Brouwer, 1946, pp. 63–66.
8. H. Urs von Balthasar, *Le Chrétien et l'Angoisse*, Paris, Desclée de Brouwer, 1954, pp. 39–40; p. 51; p. 63.
9. *Ibid.*, p. 89.
10. On imputability under stress cf. J. Ford and G. Kelly, *Contemporary Moral Theology*, Westminster, Newman, 1958, vol. i, ch. xi.
11. *Ibid.*, pp. 245–246.

CHAPTER VI: GROWTH IN CHRIST

1. K. Rahner, "Zum theologischen Begriff der Konkupiscenz," *Zeitschrift für Katholische Theologie*, 1941, pp. 71–73.
2. P. Monier, *Exercises Spirituelles*, Paris, Vitte, 1952, pp. 385–387; cf. also L. B. Geiger, "Esquisse d'une théologie de l'ascèse" in *L'Ascèse Chrétienne et l'Homme Contemporain*, Paris, Cerf, 1951, pp. 177–186.
3. Monier, *op. cit.*, p. 386.
4. A. Galtier-Sageret, "Abnégation Chrétienne," *Revue d'Ascétique et de Mystique*, 1957 (33), pp. 6–7; pp. 14–18.
5. Franssen, *art. cit.*, pp. 215–220.
6. Galtier-Sageret, *art. cit.*, p. 19.
7. *Ibid.*, p. 23. Cf. Galtier-Sageret "Abnegation et oraison," *Christus*, 1958 (17), p. 65.
8. Cf. the author's *The World to Come*, pp. 157–168.

CHAPTER VII: THE WORK OF THE CHRISTIAN

1. H. Rondet, "Eléments pour une théologie du travail," *N.R.T.*, 1955, pp. 33–35.
2. *Ibid.*, p. 39.
3. J. Husslein, *Bible and Labor*, New York, Macmillan, 1924, p. 15.
4. *Ibid.*, pp. 90–93.

5. A. de Bovis, "Le sens Catholique du travail et de la civilization," *N.R.T.*, 1950 (72), pp. 360–362.
6. Leo XIII, *Immortale Dei, D.B.*, 1879.
7. M. Guiliani, "Trouver Dieu en toutes choses," *Christus,* 1955, pp. 178–180.
8. E. Coreth, "In actione contemplativus," *Zeitschrift für Katholische Theologie,* 1956 (76), pp. 60–61.
9. *Ibid.*, p. 75.
10. Giuliani, *art. cit.*, p. 79.